GW01486183

A Waltz of Grace

A pianist's journey through hardships, her discovery of faith, and life with God

Peace be with You!

HELENA LEWIS

Cathy Theongmi Park

Copyright © 2014, 2015 Helena Lewis.

All rights reserved. No part of this book may be used or reproduced by any means, graphic, electronic, or mechanical, including photocopying, recording, taping or by any information storage retrieval system without the written permission of the author except in the case of brief quotations embodied in critical articles and reviews.

WestBow Press books may be ordered through booksellers or by contacting:

WestBow Press
A Division of Thomas Nelson & Zondervan
1663 Liberty Drive
Bloomington, IN 47403
www.westbowpress.com
1 (866) 928-1240

Because of the dynamic nature of the Internet, any web addresses or links contained in this book may have changed since publication and may no longer be valid. The views expressed in this work are solely those of the author and do not necessarily reflect the views of the publisher, and the publisher hereby disclaims any responsibility for them.

Any people depicted in stock imagery provided by Thinkstock are models, and such images are being used for illustrative purposes only.
Certain stock imagery © Thinkstock.

ISBN: 978-1-4908-7705-1 (sc)
ISBN: 978-1-4908-7704-4 (hc)
ISBN: 978-1-4908-7706-8 (e)

Library of Congress Control Number: 2015906005

Print information available on the last page.

WestBow Press rev. date: 10/12/2015

Contents

Part 1: Mirror 1
1. Wings 5
2. A Teenage Dawkins 8
3. The Silence of God 12
4. Dealing with Fear 17

Part 2: The Problem of Pain 23
5. Warning Signs 29
6. Breakout 33
7. The Unexpected 40
8. An Incident with Homeless People 45

Part 3: To England 49
9. The Wilderness Called England 53
10. A Waiting Rose 56
11. Learning Patience 60
12. The Dose of Love, Mercy, and Grace 63
13. A London University 67
14. The Pen Incident 70
15. Anne 74

Part 4: Seeing for the First Time 77
16. The Bible and Numbers 81
17. The Circumcision of the Mind 83
18. A Made-Up God? 86

19. The Name of Religion 92
20. Christianity and Other Religions 95
21. Is Christianity Self-Righteous? Discovering Faith 101
22. The Mind of God 106
23. On Happiness 112
24. The Three Temptations of Humankind 114
25. When Eve Saw the Tree 117
26. The Paradox of Life 123
27. Does the Bible Contain Errors? 129
28. The Human Error 138
29. Understanding beyond Our Dimension 145
30. God Seeks Us First 148
31. Why God Gave Us the Law 151
32. The Blood of the Cross and the Sin of Humankind 155
33. Melchizedek 160
34. Jesus' Seven Sayings upon the Cross 163
35. Standing before the Almighty 170
36. Christianity and Money 176
37. A Three-Dimensional World and Noah's Ark 179
38. Three Principles of Action 183
39. Knowledge to Eternal Life 185
40. The Purpose of Creation 189

Part 5: Reassessing the Mirror 193
41. The Wilderness Walk 197
42. Intertwined in Faith 201
43. A Blessed Life 203

Sources 205

PART ONE

Mirror

PART ONE

Mirror

I was bleeding inside the mirror. I did not feel any pain; however, after I saw myself in the mirror, I started to cry.

When I was six years old, I fell into a well and broke my nose. Thankfully, I was rescued right away, but the incident left me with a permanent scar etched on the side of my nose that remains to this day.

This is a memory from the third grade. My house had a big mirror in the living room. I enjoyed playing with the mirror, staring into the glass; the hours would simply fly by. As I stared into the glass, I always imagined there was another version of me somewhere. The reflection in the mirror never talked to me first. When I called out to her by name, the girl in the mirror never replied but only imitated my actions.

Whenever I looked into the mirror, I always thought of my friend Juni. Dressed in ragged clothes, Juni had dirty, blackened hands and a snivelly nose. I pitied her. "If my name was Juni, would I have to switch lives with her?" "If I did, then would I have to wear dirty clothes like she does?"

I envisioned Juni wearing a pretty dress while I dressed down in her ragged clothing. I called out her name as I looked into the mirror once again. Then I called out the names of other friends, too. However, when my own reflection stood there, unflinching upon the mention of all those names, I saw that it didn't matter whether my name was changed or not. I felt that my name was a fake and that my reflection in the mirror was that of a stranger whom I was seeing for the first time. Also, the world inside the mirror had no sound or sense of time. If I stared into it long enough, then I felt myself being sucked into the world where there was no sound.

We all have a mirror within our minds. It is the silhouette of our inner selves. There are many who live within the mirror of their minds in haze and bewilderment. Countless people live in confusion and self-deception. As they live their lives, they bang their fists on the glass and cry out, mistaking the reflection in the mirror for somebody else. They do not see themselves as they stand in front of God—completely hideous in wrongdoing and sin. It is my hope that when the reader looks into the mirror, his or her inner self will reflect a beautiful image in front of God.

CHAPTER 1

Wings

"My wings, my wings, won't you take flight once more?"

Like the narrator of the story "The Wings" by Yi Sang, who was struggling to make sense of his identity among his troubled life and personality issues, I thought for some time that I might be an angel who had lost her wings. Nothing in the world seemed to go my way, and my life, merely one existence among countless others, appeared insignificant and meaningless. I was an aspiring pianist but had grievously injured my fingers. I also failed to achieve my dream of entering S. University. No matter how tirelessly I worked and pushed myself, things didn't work out so easily.

At the age of six, I started taking piano lessons as a hobby. From that point onwards, my lifelong aspiration was to become a professional pianist. I was talented and quick to learn. In middle school, I performed Mozart's Piano Concerto no. 14 (K. 414) alongside a prestigious city orchestra in Korea.

Moving to Seoul after graduating from middle school, I worked towards music school and, in my final year of high school, applied to the music department of S. University, the most prestigious university in Korea. Ignoring protests from my father, who insisted that I should study business administration, I was determined to study music. But then, after my hand injury and an unexpected accident on the day of the entrance exam, my childhood dream slipped through my fingertips. I ended up enrolling in H. University instead.

Upon entering a university that I had never cared for, I felt no motivation to study. Until my third year, I paid little attention in class and practised the piano just enough to pass my practical exams. Only in my final year did I start paying more attention to my studies and dragged up my pitiful GPA to a B+. However, the fact remained that neither school life nor academics had interested me for most of my university life. I thought of my life as a complete failure. Because of this, my mind was always spewing with unrest.

When others looked at my life, they assumed that I had it all, including parents who ran a big business and provided me with every material comfort. When I looked at my life, however, I was full of discontent. I was also bad-tempered and prideful—standing up to my parents and treating people just as I wanted. My obstinacy and temper became so extreme that employees in our house threatened to resign, saying that they couldn't work because I made their jobs so difficult.

I still remember Mrs. P. A divorced woman, Mrs. P. was our housekeeper. I would call her through the speakerphone in my room, asking her to fetch me a glass of water. If she wasn't fast enough, I would reprimand her. If I found a strand of hair in my food, I would throw a fit. Whenever I couldn't find something after Mrs. P. had cleaned my room, I became absolutely enraged. I also got angry with our maid Eun-ah on a daily basis. I was ill-tempered to the point that I couldn't even understand my own anger—and I hated myself for it.

Then the unexpected struck me like lightning. With questions about the meaning of life simmering in my mind, I came to reflect upon myself and turned to the Bible. Now, when I look back on my life, I can see that everything happened under God's guidance and grace.

When I finished the Bible, I was completely transformed. It wasn't the fragmented story I had heard bits and pieces of during sermons. After reading the whole Bible, from Genesis to Revelation, I was overwhelmed by a tide of inexplicable emotions. It was an experience that opened up my eyes and ears for the first time.

The more I started to know of God's infinite and mysterious providence, the more I started to see my true reflection, a microscopic speck of dust in comparison to Him. I saw the true monster that I was, filled with greed, jealousy, avarice, pride, prejudice, selfishness, and self-righteousness. A particularly obstinate kind of monster, I took a rather long time to transform into a somewhat ordinary human being.

God pulled me out from where I had been huddling in a ditch of pride and avarice and lifted my eyes to the heavenly kingdom of humility and self-sacrifice. He bound up the hurt of my heart and healed it. Taking me in as His daughter, He dressed me in the clothes of glory and presented me with gifts of thanksgiving, love, forgiveness, and peace. When I was faced with the forgiveness and love of God, who loved me to the point of dying on the cross, even while I was in the hideous state of sin, there was no one I could not forgive.

I was able to break out of the darkness filled with hatred, prejudice, self-righteousness, arrogance, fear, avarice, and ignorance and to enter a world that was ebullient with God's light.

The Bible completely changed my former thoughts and beliefs. I felt as if the wings I had once lost had been restored. Stretching out my wings like a bird, I became a free spirit.

God finds delight in giving people the gifts of freedom and peace.

CHAPTER 2

A Teenage Dawkins

Before I encountered God's grace in my life, I was sardonic and self-centred, believing that my life was extremely unlucky. Incapable of being satisfied, I saw no such thing as thanksgiving in my life. I largely blamed God—who I wasn't even sure existed. Since my teenage years, I remember being only angry, frustrated, or dissatisfied about the state of my life, lashing out at my parents, who tried their level best to take me to church.

As I started learning about human history and theories of physics in middle school, I scoffed at the sermons I was forced to listen to when my parents dragged me to church every Sunday, convinced that they were pure nonsense.

In my teenage years, Christianity seemed like a complete fallacy. The pastors appeared completely hapless, while the Bible seemed illogical and unscientific. When I flipped through the Old Testament, I saw a two-faced, unjust God who was a narrow-minded executioner full of self-righteousness.

For instance, I was the eldest daughter of my family, but the main characters in the Bible were predominantly male. Also, the fact that the oldest child was never "chosen" by God but was always exempted from blessings seemed unfair and incomprehensible. At the time, I often wondered, *What kind of injustice is this?* Whenever I read about Cain and Abel, Jacob and Esau, Joseph and his brothers, and Manasseh and Ephraim, among others, I simply felt irritated. *Well, what am I supposed to do when I'm the eldest, too?* I thought angrily.

I also disliked the attitude and behaviour of most churchgoers, which led me to stack up only criticism against them.

As a teenager, I clung to all the prejudice and claims against Christianity that Richard Dawkins expresses today. When my parents tried to take me to church by force, I stood up to them and demanded, "Why is there no freedom of religion in this household?" The fact that I couldn't spend my Sundays catching up with schoolwork or piano practice incensed me even more. The fact that I, with work piling up each day, had to go to church and listen to some unintelligible pastor blabber away for hours incensed me and almost drove me mad. So when my parents would tell me to get ready for church, I would scream at them, saying that they would be responsible if I fell behind in my studies. Sometimes, I dreaded Sundays to the extent that I hid in the closet. When I was inevitably forced to go to church, I would close my eyes at the very beginning of the sermon and sleep through the whole thing, uncaring of what others might think or say.

Then, somehow, I ended up accompanying the choir for a couple of months. If the conductor allowed the practice session to drag on beyond the usual ending time, I expressed my discontent by slamming shut the piano lid or interrupting the choir practice by playing the hymns in a completely different key.

Once in a while, I would even pester the pastor or the elders with a bunch of questions I knew they couldn't answer. I would turn my nose up at them and ask if they knew any history or philosophy at all. I contemptuously scoffed at the Bible, laughing about how it didn't meet even the most rudimentary standards of logic. To me, it was pure drivel short of a story. For instance, how could Adam possibly be the first man when humans have existed for millions of years? The pastor could only respond by telling me, "Just believe."

I continued to badger him, asking whom God was referring to when He gave Cain a mark on his forehead so that "people he met" would not kill him after he ran away after killing his brother Abel. I further questioned the pastor. "Doesn't this logically imply that there were others living during this time when Adam was supposed to be the first man?" He could not give me an answer.

Pastors, elders, and the members of the church would whisper about me, marvelling at how such a holy elder like my father could have begotten such a Satan-like child. I remained completely unaffected by such words. When the sermon started, I would put my head on the piano lid and fall asleep in full view of everyone.

No matter what I did, no one could say anything against me because my father gave large donations in offerings, making construction projects possible for the church, and my mother had been the chairwoman of the women's ministry for years.

I did exactly as I pleased, and no one stopped me. However, I found that no matter how hard I tried, the things I desired and craved for didn't work out as I had wanted. When I failed to enter S. University, despite my all my effort, I felt as if the sky had fallen. My failure filled me with frustration and unquenchable anger. The world seemed totally unfair. From that moment on, I began to live miserably, regarding myself as a victim and a loser.

Even when I lived like a princess, being driven to school by a chauffeur—and this was during the early 1970s, when a car was a rare sight to see in the rugged Korean streets—and having maids at my beck and call, I still cursed the heavens because I was merely some faux princess instead of being the daughter of Queen Elizabeth. If God existed, then I thought He was horribly unfair to me, who deserved better.

I lived a lost and anguished life before experiencing the turbulent twist in my thirties that led me realise the meaning of grace and thanksgiving. If God had not extended His grace and love to me first, then this would not have been possible.

Karl Marx and Friedrich Nietzsche claim that humans create a god because they want something to rely on, but this is completely untrue. God was, is, and always will be alive—yesterday, today, and tomorrow. He longingly waits for us arrogant people to break out of our ignorance and self-righteousness and seek Him. When we return to Him and come to repentance, He accepts us in His infinite grace and love, giving us inexplicable joy and peace.

CHAPTER 3

The Silence of God

You believe in God playing dice, and I in perfect laws in the world of things existing as real objects, which I try to grasp in a wildly speculative way.[1]

—Albert Einstein, in a 1971 letter to Max Born

When reading the Bible, we can find certain verses that are keys to unlock the mysteries of contemporary physics or astronomy. I often think that if Albert Einstein had had a proper knowledge of the Bible, then he would have been able to complete his unified field theory.

Contemporary physics has far surpassed the theory of relativity and has even reached the understanding of the tenth dimension through the superstring theory. However, it is often the case that even a scientific genius has trouble understanding who God is. When people are hit with natural disasters or face situations that are difficult to comprehend, they ask how such things could be possible if there were a god. Also, as some look at people with birth defects or disabilities, they even mistakenly come to think that God is imperfect and makes mistakes once in a while.

These people speak as if this imperfect God rolls a die and gambles with humans. However, God is impeccable and does not make any errors or mistakes. Moreover, He is not some idle old man in the sky who rolls the dice.

There are some sudden occurrences that we cannot understand—natural disasters, deformations, mutations, and disabilities, which all entail God's deliberation and purpose.

Buddhism and Hinduism offer the concept of karma as an explanation for these kinds of phenomena. But for those who believe in God, this interpretation is inapplicable.

When Jesus' disciples asked why some people were born with defects or subject to disastrous deaths, He replied that it was "God's will."

In such an incomprehensible world, it is God's will that we give Him glory and thanks, even for the most ordinary things we take for granted.

It seems as though the mighty God who worked miracles throughout history is remaining silent for the time being. Even in human society, if there is someone who is hard to understand or get through to, the best course of action is to leave that person be for a while. Like explaining calculus to a child who has only just learned addition and subtraction, it is useless trying to explain things in a way that cannot be understood.

God is extremely patient with the ignorance of humankind. However, he will not leave us hanging forever. All things come to be under God's will. Even in situations that we can't make sense of at the time, it becomes clear after a while that there are truths He wants us to come to realise. His silence, in fact, is a distressed and desperate call to us that we cannot, or sometimes refuse to, hear.

When God was silent, I lived my life clambering in confusion, inanity, and darkness. After I hurt my nose, I studied hard to overcome my insecurity about my appearance. After playing with a famous city orchestra in middle school, I strove to achieve my dream of becoming a pianist. However, during a fire drill in the second year of high school, I had a fall that seriously injured my fingers as well as my ambitions of becoming a pianist.

But then this was nothing in comparison to an accident that happened later on. The fatal blow to all my hopes and dreams came on the very day of the entrance exam to S. University. As vehicles were not allowed in beyond the school gates, I had to walk in. During my walk was when I slipped backwards on the ice, smashing my head against the ground. However, that couldn't excuse me from taking the test. I forced myself up and took the exam, but I soon experienced terrible stomach cramps. Ten minutes before the English written exam, I had to rush to the bathroom and could not re-enter the examination room in time. I could not believe it. At a loss of what to do, I stood at the doors of the examination room, crying and crying.

To make things worse, on the day of the practical exam, I miscalculated the range of a scale and ended up playing in a completely different key. I made a mistake in a Beethoven sonata and completely butchered a Chopin etude. I had played unimaginably worse than in any of my practice sessions, yet I still held onto the hope that I had somehow passed. But, of course, I had failed. And the pain from my fall on the first day of examinations took more than a month to recede.

Right after I failed the admission exams, I made up my mind to retry for S. University even if I had to do it ten times over. However, as much as I was hot-tempered, I wasn't consistent. So I couldn't stick to this determination and ended up settling for H. University instead.

I spent my first year of university mostly reading books and shopping instead of studying for my classes. I passed my time buying pretty clothes and accessories, barely touching my piano or textbooks. However, in the second semester of my third year, I started to care about my grades and began studying intensively for my tests. When I graduated, my overall GPA had risen to a B+, but, by then, I had become sick and tired of studying.

From the moment I set foot in university, my parents started badgering me to get married because they didn't have a son. When I finally graduated, my fate became sealed almost instantly. The marriage that I was rushed into was the prologue signalling that the turbulent road of suffering in my life had just begun.

Before the unexpected happened, God was an existence that was plain burdensome to me. Through the ignorance of not knowing God, I lived my life in confusion, inanity, and darkness. Although the early years of my life spent wandering in ignorance of God were the darkest years of my soul, and although it seemed that God was silent during all that time, it was a period in which the Holy Spirit had been sorrowfully watching over me and pleading on my behalf.

Four hundred years before Jesus' birth, God had ceased speaking to the Israelite people and was silent. The last prophet was Malachi. During God's period of silence, the Israelites were spiritually dormant and couldn't understand the Bible properly. Eventually, they ended up crucifying the Messiah, Jesus, on the cross when he came, four hundred years later.

Then the good news of salvation went over the borders into the lands of strangers. When God is silent, it does not mean that we should live in defiance and according to our own desires. We must hold on to the Word and deeply contemplate what God wants, determining how we should live our lives accordingly.

As the saying goes, empty vessels make the greatest sound. With the little knowledge I had, I showed off and lived haughtily, treating others like fools. Filled to the brim with prejudice, self-righteousness, arrogance, and selfishness, I missed the chance to "remember my Creator in the days of my youth while the evil days come not." We must live a life that "remembers our Creator," instead of living idly in this hollow world that is void of meaning.

The life of a person who fails to acknowledge God's existence is unspeakably pitiful. This is because setting one's goals on the useless objects of this world and living without meaning only makes one realise the emptiness of life instead of knowing the path of blessings and what genuine happiness really is.

When it seems that God is hiding from us, it is because our eyes cannot see Him. On the other hand, if we open up our eyes, then we are able to see how He is with us and works throughout our daily lives.

Some mistake Him as an obscure God who plays hide-and-seek and gambles with human life by rolling the dice. Denying God because He has not made some extravagant, miraculous appearance is beyond foolish. It comes from ignorance that tries to make sense of the spiritual world through the five senses of the body.

God's silence is a time when the Holy Spirit pleads on behalf of ignorant humans, though with sighs and groans that cannot be expressed in words. Thus, in reality, God is not silent but is consistently and tirelessly pleading for the salvation of human souls yesterday, today, and tomorrow.

CHAPTER 4

Dealing with Fear

> So do not fear, for I am with you; do not be dismayed, for I am your God. I will strengthen you and help you; I will uphold you with my righteous right hand.
>
> —Isaiah 41:19

In the course of life, there will be many times when you bump into fear and become afraid. In my early years of adulthood, I had many fears and worries on my mind—fear of the future, sudden illness, and disastrous events. Thankfully, I came to realise that God wants people to be released from such fears and anxieties. He tells us not to be afraid. In Joshua 1 alone, the words "do not fear" are emphasised three times. The same message is reiterated throughout the rest of the Bible.

> Be strong and courageous, because you will lead these people to inherit the land I swore to their forefathers to give them. Be strong and very courageous. Be careful to obey all the law my servant Moses gave you; do not turn from it to the right or to the left, that you may be

successful wherever you go. Do not let this Book of the Law depart from your mouth; meditate on it day and night, so that you may be careful to do everything written in it. Then you will be prosperous and successful. Have I not commanded you? Be strong and courageous. Do not be terrified; do not be discouraged, for the Lord your God will be with you wherever you go. (Joshua 1:6–9)

"Be strong and courageous. Do not be afraid or terrified because of them, for the Lord your God goes with you; he will never leave you nor forsake you" (Deuteronomy 31:6).

"The Lord himself goes before you and will be with you; he will never leave you nor forsake you. Do not be afraid; do not be discouraged" (Deuteronomy 31:8).

"The Lord gave this command to Joshua son of Nun: 'Be strong and courageous, for you will bring the Israelites into the land I promised them on oath, and I myself will be with you'" (Deuteronomy 31:23).

"Do not let your hearts be troubled. Trust in God; trust also in me" (John 14:1).

I have had many fears since I was a little girl. I couldn't leave the house at night, because I was afraid of the dark. I remember walking down an alleyway with my sister one evening. Feeling that something was pulling me from the back as if to snatch me, I walked hurriedly in front of her. When I became afraid of watching TV in my room, I hid under the duvet and remained fully covered as I stumbled over to turn off the set.

Even in university, where I was forced to socialise with others, I rarely went out at night and kept the lights on as I slept. The cinema also unsettled me, so I never went to the movies other than those I had to watch during school trips in middle school. I was even afraid of dogs. That was why I would glare at the dogs' owners before I ran away. But then when I saw someone hurting a dog, I couldn't stand it, even in my fear. I would shout at the abuser for hurting an ignorant creature that couldn't even speak; then, I would flee from the scene. The world was like a chamber filled with horrors. I gradually closed myself up in an isolated chamber of my own.

In the summer of 1981, the year of Prince Charles and Diana Spencer's wedding, I went on a foreign-exchange programme with students from K. University. I enrolled in a college in Cambridge to take a language course abroad. In those days, there weren't any planes that went straight to England, so I had to go through Hong Kong in transit. It was a long journey. I spent a night in Hong Kong before going to Bahrain to get a flight to London. Once I arrived at London Heathrow, I had to travel up to Cambridge to go to my assigned university. When I got to the school, the dormitory had filled up, so they were assigning the remaining students to host families. They told us that if we didn't like our host family, we could switch to another house. The office woman in the school administration introduced me to a young, pretty woman called Laura. As Laura drove me to her place, I was bursting with curiosity. Wanting to know what kind of house it was and how English people lived, I was full of excitement.

When I arrived at her house, I saw a huge black dog the size of a small cow. Then, the man whom Laura introduced as her husband had a stern face and was about twice the size of my small Korean father; furthermore, he sported a stark blue tattoo on his shoulder. In those days, tattoos were quite rare in Korea, so the sight of this one instantaneously frightened me. Seeing the couple's two-year-old daughter was the only thing that reassured me. Even so, I felt that it was impossible to settle in this contrary place. I told Laura I would just drop by school, but I packed up all my bags to leave. I retraced on foot the track I had come by car, staggering as I went, and somehow got myself back on campus.

I went straight to the administration office and begged them to change my host family. After making several phone calls, the office woman pulled a face, telling me that it would be extremely difficult to make changes at that point. My heart dropped to the ground. No matter how much I begged and pleaded, there wouldn't be a house I could immediately stay in. There was no choice but to go back to Laura's house. Tears clouded the road ahead of me as I carried back all my bags. Crying as I went, I found myself at Laura's front door again. During the three weeks that I spent there, I always slept with the lights on.

When classes were over at the university, I found returning home to be a true terror. By the time the lectures ended around 5:00 p.m., the sky was already pitch-black, not to mention that there were only a few people walking on the roads, where there were no streetlights.

Although I always stuck to the side of the road where houses were lit up and ran home as if fleeing for my life, I still felt afraid. One day, I was standing alone by the school gates, tearing up at the thought of my parents back in Korea and my chauffeur who had always picked me up from school. Cambridge was a rural area, so there weren't any taxis driving down the roads. If I wanted to get a taxi, then I would have to call one out by making a reservation. Not only was the procedure cumbersome, but also there was something about English taxi drivers that scared me. I just stood at the gate homesick and crying when M., my professor, walked by and stopped short to ask me why I was crying. Blubbering, I told him I was afraid of the dark and had no idea how to get home. From that day onwards, he drove me all the way to Laura's house each day until the language course ended.

The other students on the exchange programme roamed around town day and night with no problems. As for me, I went straight home after class and read books or played with Laura's little girl. I couldn't understand why anyone would go out late at night.

Before I read the Bible, I lived in sheer terror and had all kinds of fear. However, as I began to read the Bible word by word, passage by passage, these worries completely disappeared. With thoughts like, *With God on my side, what could possibly happen to me?* and *How can I, a daughter of God, be afraid of a mere dog or the existence of ghosts?*, I started to become fearless. Even to me, this was an unbelievable transformation. Not only that, but I even stopped being afraid of failure. This difference in me was incomparable to the time when I didn't know God. I realised that God's greatest gift is peace of mind.

As we live, we fret over small illnesses, worrying and fearing that they may be chronic diseases. Many people continue to carry a huge sack of fear and worry on their backs even though they claim to believe in God. Fear derives from the lack of complete faith in God. As long as we are afraid, our minds cannot be happy, peaceful, and at rest. However, God tells us humans that we no longer have to be afraid of anything. It is not His intention for people to live shaking in the shadows of fear and tied down to sin like slaves. God wants people to enjoy free and happy lives. "Peace I leave with you; my peace I give you. I do not give to you as the world gives. Do not let your hearts be troubled and do not be afraid" (John 14:27).

We must not be afraid or worry about anything; instead, we must live each and every day on the earth in prayer and thanksgiving to God. For us who believe in God, nothing can make us afraid, whether it is a certain person or a situation.

> "In God I trust; I will not be afraid. What can man do to me" (Psalm 56:11)?

> "Do not be anxious about anything, but in everything, by prayer and petition, with thanksgiving, present your requests to God" (Philippians 4:6).

> I lift up my eyes to the hills where does my help come from? My help comes from the Lord, the Maker of heaven and earth. He will not let your foot slip he who watches over you will not slumber; indeed, he who watches over Israel will neither slumber nor sleep. The Lord watches over you, the Lord is your shade at your right hand; the

sun will not harm you by day, nor the moon by night. The Lord will keep you from all harm, he will watch over your life; the Lord will watch over your coming and going both now and forevermore. (Psalm 121)

PART TWO

The Problem of Pain

PART TWO

The Problem of Pain

> What is man that you make so much of him, that you give him so much attention, that you examine him every morning and test him every moment?
>
> —Job 7:17–18

After I graduated from university and embarked upon my adult life, a series of calamities tumbled down on me like a ton of bricks. Things I could have never expected or imagined, even among my compulsive worrying, led me through the years of pain and suffering.

Only through pain can a person mature. When such a person looks back, years later, he or she comes to know that the suffering was not in vain. Through the time of suffering, one develops a more profound mind of reason and comes to realise one's true identity. As the saying goes, it takes knowledge to play the part. When humans wake up from their spiritual slumber and ignorance, they start to know God empirically through their own experience. The more profound this experience is, the more they can grow in maturity upon the certainty of their faith.

That is how we can say that the problem of pain and suffering is ultimately God's providence for bringing about inner maturity. Through suffering, humans come face-to-face with the complex problems that life entails. However, the foundational question about humans cannot easily be posed without experiencing inner pain. C. S. Lewis said in *The Problem of Pain* that "God whispers to us in our pleasures, speaks in our conscience, but shouts in our pain: it is His megaphone to rouse a deaf world."[1]

In reality, it is God who hurts the most when we suffer. When we are in pain, God is there with us and feels every single ache along with us. "In all their distress he too was distressed, and the angel of his presence saved them. In his love and mercy he redeemed them; he lifted them up and carried them all the days of old" (Isaiah 63:9).

Although we are unsure of what to do and cannot even lift up our hands in prayer, the Holy Spirit takes our place and pleads for our souls with groaning inexpressible in words. Like a distressed parent who disciplines his child, God's heart breaks for us when we are in pain. That is why we shouldn't fall into hopelessness or complaint in a time of suffering, but take on a humble attitude in which we pray to God, seeking His help.

> Keep your lives free from the love of money and be content with what you have, because God has said, "Never will I leave you; never will I forsake you." So we say with confidence, "The Lord is my helper; I will not be afraid. What can man do to me?" Remember your leaders, who spoke the word of God to you. Consider the outcome of their way of life and imitate their faith. Jesus Christ is the same yesterday and today and forever. (Hebrews 12:5–13)

Most people are stricken with fear and hurt by the kaleidoscopic problems that life throws at them, but the solution is surprisingly simple. Whatever troubles we may face, all we must do is return to God—and the problem is resolved. The answer to life is to find God because in Him lie all the solutions. "'For I know the plans I have for you,' declares the Lord, 'plans to prosper you and not to harm you, plans to give you hope and a future. Then you will call upon me and come and pray to me, and

I will listen to you. You will seek me and find me when you seek me with all your heart'" (Jeremiah 29:11–13).

God does not reject those who seek Him. If we call out to Him in times of trouble, He will come to us. Thus, when we are suffering, we must seek Him with all our strength. It is then that our problems will be solved, as our times of suffering change into turning points for blessings.

CHAPTER 5

Warning Signs

> What is man that you make so much of him, that you give him so much attention, that you examine him every morning and test him every moment?
>
> —Job 7:17–18

Engaged at twenty-three and married at twenty-four, I found that my married life proved to be extremely difficult from the very start. My younger brother had died when he was five years old, so my parents, who were left without a son, pressured me to marry straight out of university so that they would have a son-in-law. From the moment I received my acceptance letter from H. University, my father began a series of lectures, pressing me to get engaged in my second year and married in my third. Every other week, I came home to find a potential suitor sitting in my living room. I marched straight into my room without even looking at these young men.

Then, one day in the beginning of my third year, I met a young man called C. For a year, he pursued me and even wrote letters to me while he was in the military. In the beginning, I rejected him flatly, but as time went on, my heart opened to him. When I told my father about C., he was overjoyed and asked to see him straightaway. As my parents had so fervently desired, I found myself engaged a month before my graduation.

However, this whirlwind bliss did not last long into my marriage. A month after the wedding, my husband was out with his friends every other night, going to bars and staying out late. Up to this point, my material life had been like Cinderella's ball, filled with riches, buoyance, and comfort. However, the promise of married bliss swept away like the wind and the flare I had as a girl flickered out completely, not to mention that my mother-in-law was a woman who would have put Cinderella's stepmother to shame. Through my years of marriage, I found myself naked and exposed, as everything I had known was torn into rags.

I had trouble adjusting to the chores that were part of married life. Slicing up beef, for instance, felt horrid and disgusting. I wondered why I had to do such cruel and vile things just to put food on the table. When the cooks back at my parents' home laid out the dishes of meat, such as bulgogi, beef soup, and barbeque, on the table, I relished the food without a single thought. But now that I was cutting up raw meat with my own bare hands, I felt sickened and completely lost my appetite.

In my premarital life, I had never once cooked a meal for anyone, nor had I cleaned my own room. Before I got married, my maids had done every task for me, from great to small. But now that I had to do things for myself, I felt as if I was going crazy. In the face of these new challenges, I started to despise my own uselessness. After only a couple of days of being married, I could no longer stand it and hired a maid. However, when she went home for the day, I felt helpless once again.

Barely in control of my own life, I had to handle the daily dramas that my in-laws threw at me. I had grown up praised and spoiled by everyone around me. In my marital life, however, no matter how hard I worked or tried to please people, I was constantly criticised and sworn at. At home, I would shout and vent out my anger, but at my husband's house, I was shrunken and speechless, meekly taking in all the criticism and profanities thrown at me.

A Waltz of Grace

In case I had done something wrong, I took great pains to treat my in-laws as well as I could. Even so, I was never good enough for them. One time, my sister-in-law hurled her gift onto the floor because I was late to her birthday party and furiously demanded to know why a young woman like me needed maids. She ordered me to make kimchi and beef stew for her and to send her kid to a private institution, among countless other demands.

Meanwhile, my mother-in-law wanted to know why a rich businessman like my father couldn't even buy his eldest daughter a house to live in. She poured out swearwords at me, her daughter-in-law who had not yet reached the first month of marriage. "Your father is an elder? Well, we're all Buddhists here, so you come here now and bow down." I had heard that women usually don't have to bow when offering a sacrifice, but my mother-in-law forced it upon me anyway while letting my brother-in-law's wife off.

Without hesitating, I answered, "Of course, Mother. My father goes to church, but I'm not a Christian." I bowed down as she had told me to, desperate to please. Not only that but every holiday I would have to prepare the food for the altar.

Every month, I supplied my in-laws with several thousand dollars of allowance. When I heard that my brother-in-law was in debt because of his drinking, I immediately withdrew ten thousand dollars from my account. However, my in-laws, whom I treated like gods, repaid me only with pain and abuse, always ready to cut me down.

The most unnerving day came about a month after my wedding. I was cleaning the house when my mother-in-law arrived unannounced. Throwing down her small, battered sack, she began to shout, "Daughter of a salesman, worthless girl from Gyeongsang [Province], what do you take us for? Who do you think you are, forgetting your sister's birthday?"

I was so alarmed that I got into a taxi and went to my sister-in-law's house right away. Once I arrived, I kneeled on the floor, pleading for her forgiveness, although I had no clue what was going on. Then my nephew came home from elementary school and my mother-in-law shouted at me, "Why on earth is she crying? What good did you do? Be quiet, you idiot. You're scaring him!" I never felt more shaken than I did in that moment. I felt as if I were about to faint. Along with my marriage, a completely new world had dawned upon my life. I started to lose heart in everything.

My so-called husband proved to be no comfort from the very start. He was now living the high life, taking advantage of my family's affluent lifestyle and spending my father's money. In the early days of our marriage, he asked my father to buy him a car—a Royal Saloon or a Jeep. My father initially refused, but as my husband angrily demanded that we should have a car, I stormed into my parents' house and threw a tantrum until my father conceded.

My father bought us the car and even gave my husband a monthly allowance that was double the average salary at the time. Within two months, C. even received a place in my father's company as director.

While working at my father's company, my husband was consistently late to work or absent, yet he took his monthly pay without fail. He would go out at night and stay out until dawn with his friends, waking up midmorning to eat before leaving for work.

He travelled to Europe for a month, telling my father that whereas I had travelled abroad since the time I was in school, he had never been overseas. "Father, my wife has been in and out of the country since her school years, but I've never been abroad once. Please, let me go, too." Then he dismissed my uncles, cousins, and other family members working in my father's company. At the top level of the company, he actually appeared to be working quite hard.

As for me, my life had become a living nightmare. The life I had before, where I was taken care of and was free to play the piano or read books, seemed like a completely different world.

CHAPTER 6

Breakout

One day in April 1994, I drove to the airport with my daughter, who had just turned one. I had gone there unplanned, feeling guilty that I hadn't picked up my husband from the airport for quite some time when he came back from business trips.

After we had been married a couple of years, my husband began to take his job more seriously. He cleared the office of my father's relatives and became the president, after convincing my father to leave the work to him and start enjoying life more with travel, golf, and other leisurely activities while remaining the chairman. After that, most of the positions in the company were filled with my husband's family members, friends, and acquaintances.

My husband was often away on business trips to Europe and America. His schedule was irregular. One time, I called his office because I didn't know when he was coming home. His assistant informed me he would be returning that day. She also told me that he had told the staff not to pick him up, which was why no one had gone to the airport. Wondering what I should do, I finally decided to pick him up at the airport. I left home for the terminal with my daughter.

At the arrivals gate, I stood far towards the back, waiting to surprise C., as I held our child in my arms. Then, I finally spotted him coming out of the doors. But then I saw him looking left and right carefully, as though he were being watched. All of a sudden, a feeling of unease entered my chest. I decided to remain out of sight just to see what was going on. Soon enough, I saw a woman with long hair start to follow my husband.

At first, there was considerable distance between the two of them, but gradually the space closed up and they began to walk together. I didn't know why, but my heart started beating quickly. The woman was holding the designer bag I had asked my husband to buy for me in Italy.

Then, in front of the taxi stop, my husband and the woman stopped short. As if the people around them were invisible, they started to kiss passionately. This was in broad daylight, in conservative Korea.

The taxi drivers around me were staring at them, nudging each other and sniggering with embarrassed expressions. I found myself marching up to the two who were in a passionate embrace. Then, I drew close to my husband and began to speak in a low voice, right into his ear. "I just can't believe this!"

My husband was frightened out of his wits and stood there dumbfounded while the woman stared at me vacantly, completely unaware of what was going on.

Soon enough, the people around us began to tut their tongues as they worked out the situation. All of a sudden, I felt humiliated. I signalled a taxi, completely forgetting that my own car was sitting in the car park. As I stumbled in, I saw the woman get into a taxi in front of me. My husband tried to get in the car with me, opening the door, but I slammed it shut.

The taxi that the woman was in began to drive off. My taxi driver, who had been standing outside watching the whole humiliating scene, looked at me through the rear-view mirror.

"Should I follow that woman?" he asked.

"Why?" I asked, taken aback.

"Well, you have find out what kind of woman she is, where she lives. You can't just leave her to it. If I were you, I'd be ripping her hair out. I don't get how you can be so calm. I think you must be crazy or else you were brought up too proper."

He was wrong in both instances, but I told him to follow her anyway.

It wasn't ten minutes before the woman's taxi pulled over and she got out of the car. "Go follow her right now. I'll be right here," the driver urged me. With my daughter in my arms, I caught up with the woman.

"Excuse me!"

The woman swivelled around.

"Excuse me. I'm the wife of that man you were with. Could I just ask you something?"

The woman stood still, silent. But as for me, the words shot out of my mouth in a single breath. "Look. I can handle pretty much anything except curiosity. What university did you go to?" She didn't respond, so I asked again. "Look, I don't care what's going on between you and that man. I told you I can't stand not knowing something. So answer me. If you don't answer me, I'm going to follow you home and tell your parents everything you've done. So answer me! What university did you go to?"

When I think about it now, I see that it was obviously a ridiculous question. But the first thing I wanted to know about the woman was what university she was from. After that, I wanted to know how she began seeing my husband, what her age was, and what her occupation was.

She stammered out answers to all my questions. Her name was M. She was aged twenty-eight, from D. University with a degree in decorative art, currently working as a display manager in a clothing company.

As for how she and my husband began their affair, that answer was simply unbelievable. Lee, a friend of my husband working as a producer in a broadcasting company, had set up blind dates for married men he knew. So my husband, along with a couple of his friends—including a friend who was on the police force—had gone along with the dates and even exchanged contact details with the women afterwards.

My husband spent money without restraint, which made him very popular with his friends. He would randomly shower them with expensive gifts—brand new cars, TVs, and electronic goods. He even bought sets of golf clubs for his friends' wives. He travelled exclusively first class or business class, all charged to my father's company. He regularly switched cars and dressed from head to toe in luxury brands and accessories.

When I got home, my husband had already arrived. As soon as he saw me, he began to drivel out all sorts of excuses that didn't make sense. By now, I knew the whole story, but as he swore that he would never see the woman again, I decided to trust him and let it go. This was in early 1993.

Even after that fateful day, my husband continued to go on business trips and stay out all night. He was home only two or three days a month, but I simply thought that he was working extremely hard.

Soon, six months had passed. One morning in 1994, I was reading the *Dong-A Ilbo,* a daily Korean newspaper. There was a short article that day about a woman named M. who had been caught at an international airport abroad, in possession of a handgun. Her male companion was unnamed.

My heart began to pound. My husband had been on a business trip in that specific city and, for some reason, had kept delaying his return. I just knew this M. had to be that woman. With this conviction, I set off for my sister-in-law's apartment with my daughter. I told my sister-in-law that I thought the woman named M. in the papers today had to be *that woman* and that my husband's delay in coming home was related to the handgun incident.

My sister-in-law looked at me straight in the eyes. "You really do have the most colourful imagination," she told me before explaining to me that I must be wrong. She ranted that the M. woman in the papers was most definitely not the same person I had seen six months ago with my husband.

Even so, I confronted my husband the next day when he arrived in Seoul, asking him if he had been delayed because he and *that woman* had been carrying a gun. I asked him point-blank if they had been the two people in the article in *Dong-A Ilbo* the previous day. My husband adamantly denied my accusations. Jumping up in indignation, he told me that I was crazy and needed to be put in a mental hospital.

Still, my heart told me I was right. I just lacked the solid evidence to prove it. Suppressing my dubious mind, I tried to bury these thoughts for about a month, but it came to a point where I couldn't hold it in any longer. One evening, I made an international phone call to the airport police at the airport mentioned in the news article. A policeman picked up, and I asked him if it was true that a Korean woman named M. had been held there.

The man answered me in a British accent, "Yes."

Then, I asked him if the man who had been accompanying her was called C. There was a pause. He finally asked me, "Who are you?"

"I'm C.'s wife," I said, before repeating my question.

"I can't answer that," he replied.

"If you don't answer me now, I am going to fly there first thing tomorrow and do whatever it takes to find out the truth!" With that, I asked him again, "Was the man with her called C.? If you really don't want to say it, then just say yes or no!"

"Yes."

At that moment, I felt the skies falling down on me. I was shaking so severely that I couldn't hold myself up.

I called my sister-in-law to tell her that everything I'd suspected was true.

She came right away. Telling me that I was shaking badly and needed something warm to drink, she actually boiled me a cup of water. I reached out to take the cup from her, but it slipped from my shaking hands and smashed onto the floor.

My sister-in-law soon left. I called my husband, who was drinking at a bar. When I said I had something to tell him and asked him to come home quickly, he told me he didn't want to right now. It wasn't that he couldn't come home; he just didn't want to. If he didn't come home, I said, then I would just have to divorce him.

After a long while, my husband walked in through the front door. "This is how I am. If you don't understand me, then let's just get a divorce." I had completely given up at this point. I decided I wanted the same thing.

However, later, when my husband got back from his sister's house, he suddenly started pleading with me for forgiveness, saying he was in the wrong. Even so, I had made up my mind. Eventually, my husband's entire family—his parents, elder brother, and sisters—found out about the situation and began to plead with me on his behalf, blaming themselves for his mistakes. They importunately tried to persuade me to take him back, saying that I would be blessed if I did so.

At this point, my mind was extremely uneasy. Suddenly, all I wanted to do was read the Bible. So I just grabbed one in the house that I had barely touched before and flipped it open. It randomly opened up to Exodus, so that was where I started to read. As I read about the Israelites who had come out of Egypt, it occurred to me that this was my own story.

I couldn't stop my tears from flowing. Beginning the very next day, as soon as my maid came in the morning, I would have her play with my daughter until dark while I read through the whole Bible for fourteen days straight. The tears continued to fall. I saw myself in the defiant Israelites. The God of Moses was not buried in the past. All this time, I had extinguished the very existence of God in my mind and had selected the path of denial, of disbelief.

Also, I realised that God is a powerful God who is the same yesterday, today, and forever. Even if I continued to deny Him out of my own ignorance, saying I didn't know Him, He knew the very depths of my heart and mind more than I myself ever could.

After spilling hot tears of repentance, I found myself going to church on my own two feet. I, who had once unforgivingly cursed anyone who dared to wake me from my sleep during services, started getting up before dawn to go to the early morning service every day. I poured out my troubles to one of the chaplains at church who urged me not to get a divorce. Forgiving my husband, she said, was something I should do without question, as I had received God's love. Upon her advice, I issued my husband an ultimatum. Only on the condition that he and his entire family go to church would I change my mind on getting a divorce.

His family members all promised to do what I said. For some time, it looked as if everything had settled back into place.

Then, several months later, a most unexpected tragedy swept over my life.

CHAPTER 7

The Unexpected

On the morning of January 29, 1995, the postman delivered a registered letter from court. "For the reasons that the defendant squanders money in extravagance and vanity, spending money as if were tap water and travelling abroad every other day, makes this marriage impossible to continue, thus I request a divorce. Plaintiff C ..."

Whereas my husband was the one who had squandered his father-in-law's money with "extravagance and luxury," he put the blame on me, stating in the documents that I had been the one to recklessly waste money. After the gun incident, he told me he would go to England to clear his head. When he returned after two months, he barely came home at all, only dropping by once in a while to take his golf membership card, some paintings, and several other things, one by one. I simply thought he was putting them in his office, but there was an underlying motive for his actions. He took all the assets he could seize in advance and then requested a divorce.

My parents were devastated. Stupefied. When I went to their house, I found a book titled *Divorce and Law* lying on the desk. I took it home to read and found that there were several important conditions for divorce. Except for the condition about three or more years of absence, they were all terms that my husband could be charged for. Crimes such as inappropriate actions, abuse of the spouse and immediate family, and abuse of the spouse's parents all applied to my husband.

I hired the best solicitor known in Seoul, and my father issued a civil suit.

The divorce suit dragged on for three years, during which time my husband and I did not exchange a single word. I found out later that he had been living with another woman the entire time, even before the divorce was finalised. In early 1998, after years of no contact, I received a sudden phone call from him. Saying that his company was in great trouble, he gave all sorts of pathetic excuses. "Even if you win this settlement, there's nothing in it for you, anyway." Then he asked to meet so that we could talk things through.

At the time, I was in the beginning stages of my spiritual life and had the passion of a new believer, deeply absorbed in and moved by grace. The fact that my husband failed to reach the most basic form of human character, with a sinful soul full of materialistic avarice and with no regard for his children, made him appear pathetic and pitiful to my eyes.

A few days after his call, I met my husband at the appointed place and asked him what he wanted. Saying that all we had to do was split the property between us, he spoke as if he was being extremely gracious by returning my own father's estate that had been placed under his name.

Up to that point, I had been struggling to decide whether it was right for me to fight for earthly possessions when I believed in God. Even if I were to win the lawsuit, in the case that the company went bankrupt, I would only be left with the hollow shell of an empty victory. That was why I only requested my little girl's child maintenance fees. In return for this, I gave my husband an estate that had remained under my name, allowing him the settlement that he wanted.

After that, I told my husband I hoped he would believe in God, repent for stealing my parents' assets, and become a new person before he died. Although he was shameless enough to trade the custody of our daughter for a building that was under my name, I went along with the settlement and stamped my seal on the documents the very next day in court.

My parents almost exploded with fury because I had allowed a settlement that gave away the rest of what we had instead of recovering our assets. I retorted that three years of brawling in the courtroom with this unbeliever had been a waste of time and money, saying that even if we were to win the case, it would be a sour victory since my husband's brother, a financial expert, as well as his other connections, would have already dealt with all the assets.

Although I couldn't utter a peep against other people in general, it was a completely different story when it came to my parents, whom I treated like dirt. I was simply a two-faced monster.

For a while after my divorce, I struggled to make sense of what Jesus had said about divorce in Matthew 19: "Moses permitted you to divorce your wives because your hearts were hard. But it was not this way from the beginning." As I read this passage, I was consumed with worry about whether I had committed a sin by getting a divorce.

However, I received a response from God. The words "other than sexual immorality" caught my eye (Matthew 19:9). There was an exception.

Since my husband had been the one to commit adultery, I felt my mind ease: I had done nothing to be held accountable for.

Also, God had not matched me with my husband. Growing up, I had always wanted to live alone. I had never had the faith or the wish to pray for a partner. That was why I never prayed, let alone even thought to consider what God had in store for me.

Before getting married, instead of looking at the physical aspects based on worldly values, people must evaluate whether the person they are committing themselves to will help build up the life of holiness that God desires. But I hadn't done this in any way.

I had been uncertain about divorce, but as these thoughts occurred to me, my mind began to ease. It was as though God had given me an exodus from living monotonously, enslaved within the spinning wheel of life. He had freed me from living as a slave to my own double personality—acting like a complete monster to my parents, but meek and unable to say a peep to my in-laws.

What I am most thankful for is the fact that God didn't reject me even to the end. Also, when I had the chance to offer forgiveness, He gave me the courage to tell my in-laws about the gospel, which compensated for the cost of my blood.

The fact that I had told my in-laws, to whom I had never dared even express the slightest will of my own, "I will forgive everything and not file for divorce if you believe in God and go to church," was an opportunity given to me by God me so that I could clear the price of my blood for failing to spread the news to those around me.

Even though my husband had used the time of grace to snatch away all my assets with an extremely ironic lawsuit, compared to how the price of my soul was cleared, the material things I lost amounted to nothing.

> Son of man, I have made you a watchman for the house of Israel; so hear the word I speak and give them warning from me. When I say to a wicked man, "You will surely die," and you do not warn him or speak out to dissuade him from his evil ways in order to save his life, that wicked man will die for his sin, and I will hold you accountable for his blood. But if you do warn the wicked man and he does not turn from his wickedness or from his evil ways, he will die for his sin; but you will have saved yourself. Again, when a righteous man turns from his righteousness and does evil, and I put a stumbling block before him, he will die. Since you did not warn him, he will die for his sin. The righteous things he did will not be remembered, and I will hold you accountable for his blood. But if you do warn the righteous man not to sin and he does not sin, he will surely live because he took warning, and you will have saved yourself. (Ezekiel 3:17–21)

Oh, how thankful I was! The unexpected had not been a curse but a blessing in disguise. I may have lost the world, but my soul had gained salvation through the unexpected catastrophe.

Even if a person is a lost soul, if he or she goes back to Him, then God will completely restore everything that had been hurt and broken. "Then the Lord your God will restore your fortunes and have compassion on you and gather you again from all the nations where he scattered you. Even if you have been banished to the most distant land under the heavens, from there the Lord your God will gather you and bring you back" (Deuteronomy 30:3–4).

CHAPTER 8

An Incident with Homeless People

In mid-1998, the president of a nongovernmental organization asked me to offer my property as a centre for educating homeless people in the city. It hadn't been long since I had gotten divorced, and I was in a state of complete exhaustion.

When the divorce suit had started, I had gone back to my parents' house to live with them. During that time, I had signed over an arcade building without my parents' permission and even had the litigation instigated by my father dismissed by agreeing to get a divorce of mutual consent. My parents were absolutely livid.

Earnestly willing to help the people in need, I granted permission for the foundation to use the property, which legally belonged to me. My parents protested, telling me I had to rent it out since we no longer had a source of income after their businesses had been taken from them. However, I refused to listen to them, arguing that God wanted me to help others.

My parents were enraged at my words, but I wouldn't back down.

Then, residents in the surrounding area began protesting against the settlement of homeless people. Friction grew between the two parties. The residents even sent a petition to the Blue House. The problem became so serious that the homeless people and the residents started getting into physical fights.

For almost a month, armed policeman had to be mobilised every day to break up fights between the residents and homeless people, who continued to hit out at each other all the way to the police station. My building became hideously covered in red graffiti. When this incident was broadcast on the three major TV networks in Korea during July of 1998, I became a public disgrace, turned out by my parents and even by my own neighbours.

The building had originally belonged to my parents, but it was under my name on paper. After my conviction of faith, I believed that everything on earth belonged to God; although something was in my possession, it wasn't truly mine. Instead, I should share it with those in need. This was the reason why I had gone against the wishes of my parents, who wanted me to rent the building out, and signed the contract that converted the building to an education centre for the homeless.

I told my parents that it was now time for us to let others have the goods we had enjoyed until now. I stubbornly argued with them.

Even then, as I went on and on about what God wanted, I failed to realise that He was the God of law and order. I disobediently fought with my parents with the conviction that I must help the poor no matter what, in any way possible. Finally, I was turned out of the house. To stop my parents from throwing me out, I stuck my leg inside the front gate, but my mother, being stronger back then, shoved me back and shut the door in my face. In resignation, I moved from hotel to hotel, later drifting around here and there.

Meanwhile, crowds of residents assembled each day in dozens and brandished their sticks to fight with the homeless people. An entire busload of policeman had to be dispatched each day to quell them.

One time, when I went near a building outside of which the residents were protesting, I ended up running away from a whole bunch of them who came after me. Some of the protestors leapt onto my car and hung onto the boot as I tried to drive away.

As the protests dragged on, the chief police officer went to my parents' house to plead with them to track their daughter down and persuade her to put an end to the situation. Absolutely clueless of my location, my parents were in a state of distress, almost to the point of losing their minds, as the residents stood outside their gates in uproar every day, protesting and shouting.

Oblivious to what my parents were going through, I spent a month wandering until I thought about going to my cousin's house. As soon as I entered through the door, my cousin demanded, "Where have you been all this time?" and told me how a huge group of residents had all-night sit-ins outside my parents' estate, even in the rain, the shock of which had almost driven my weak-hearted father to the grave.

My cousin phoned my parents immediately. I ended up going home. I realised that no matter how charitable donating my property would be, I could no longer go ahead with this cause with so many people in protest and when my parents were so dead-set against it. I signed the documents terminating the deal, and the crisis was over.

Going through this situation, I felt huge disappointment and disillusionment towards both the residents and the homeless people. Witnessing the residents who had opposed the move in case their property values would go down and the homeless people rising up to strike in violent protest, occupying the building, and starting fights, I witnessed the pure greed and selfishness of humans and became disheartened. After the incident with the homeless people, I didn't want to be in Korea a second longer. I decided to study abroad in England.

PART THREE

To England

PART THREE

To England

In the 1980s, Chun Doo-hwan, a former military officer, became president of Korea. Overseas travel became open to the public. I had always fantasised about travelling to Europe, so I begged my parents to let me go that very summer. I spent my first two weeks in England, where I took a language course. For the rest of the summer, I visited Italy, France, Germany, and Switzerland. These days, you can get to Europe the very same day, as a plane trip takes only about twelve hours, but back then it was a long journey: I had to take the Cathay Pacific to Hong Kong, where I spent the night before going to Bahrain to get another plane to England.

If I were to sum up my experience in each European country, I would say that throughout this vacation, I realised I had been like a frog trapped in a well.

Korea, with its five thousand years of rich history and its mountaintops that are beautiful in all four seasons, all of a sudden seemed like a small and shabby place.

Thanks to images in the media, I had a rough sketch of what the outside world must look like, but as I saw Europe through my own eyes, my country shamefully didn't even come close. Never mind the fact that my country had a backward economy after the Korean War— the differences in perception and values between the two countries made Koreans seem like barbarians in comparison to the educated and culturally sophisticated Western people. Korea seemed to be lagging a hundred years behind.

It was then that I promised myself that I would live in Europe one day. From this point on, I travelled to Europe whenever I could find the occasion.

I visited England several times after that first, eye-opening summer vacation, but when I went there to study in 1998, I chose England not only because it was familiar to me, but also because it was the home of many great people I admired. As the motherland of James Clerk Maxwell, Steven Hawking, and Paul Davies, among many eminent others, England seemed more of an attractive place to live than any other European country.

When I left for England, I told myself that I would cultivate myself with Western education and somehow become a force for change in this unfair, corrupted world. It was only later that I realised that it was not the world but my own self I had to change.

CHAPTER 9

The Wilderness Called England

> Remember how the Lord your God led you all the way in the desert these forty years, to humble you and to test you in order to know what was in your heart, whether or not you would keep his commands.
>
> —Deuteronomy 8:2

When my daughter and I started our life in England in August 1998, it was completely different from the times when I had come to stay on vacations. Previously on my occasional visits to London, I had stayed at luxurious hotels like the Ritz or the Dorchester, and I had even become familiar with the staff, who recognised me years after my last stay.

Now, it was completely different. After losing almost everything I had, I couldn't afford to spend a single night in the hotels that I was used to. I had to look for alternatives. Turning up my nose at the odour and stuffiness of three-star hotels, I checked into four-star places like the Rembrandt near Harrods Department Store.

Discovering that paying rent would be much cheaper than staying at a hotel, I, with my daughter in two, started searching for flats at local real-estate agencies. I chose to live in the Chelsea neighbourhood, afraid to leave the vicinity of Ritz Hotel. After a year of living in Chelsea, however, I found that thousands of pounds had evaporated from my account. Even so, I didn't think of living anywhere else and was wondering what I should do. One day, as I was going back to my flat, I saw a male uniformed worker leave my flat. Startled, I went to straight to the building's office.

I lived in a residential suite where the other half of the block ran as a hotel. The rooms on the hotel side could be accessed with the master key, but my flat was a personal residence, so I demanded to know how the worker had gotten in.

The receptionist told me that the worker must have gotten mixed up and gone into the wrong room. Even so, the suspicion remained, lingering in my mind.

Then, by chance, I heard that a friend from university had come to London because of her husband's work and was living in New Malden, a town where many Koreans lived. Pleasantly surprised, I contacted Y. and arranged to go to her house to visit. She told me that I just had to go down to Wimbledon, where she'd pick me up in her car. As I rarely left the Chelsea area, I felt slightly nervous every time the train for Wimbledon passed by the platform, as if I were getting farther from the city just by looking at the train. But then, as I looked around New Malden, I noticed that the town seemed tidy and comfortable enough to live in. So I decided to move there rather than live in the city, where living expenses were sky-high in comparison. That was when my life in England really started.

It was the first Sunday in New Malden after moving there. With my daughter, I walked to a Korean church that was close to our house. I was standing by the entrance, skimming over the church bulletin, when the pastor's name caught my eye. His surname was C., the same as my ex-husband's! Shoving the leaflet back in its place, I took my daughter home without a single glance over my shoulder. I'd told myself I had forgiven my ex-husband, but when it came down to reality, my blood boiled even at hearing his surname.

When I had last seen him at the divorce settlement, I had said that through the grace of God, I would "just trust in Him, although everything has been taken from me." But then, as I started my new life with a shortage of money, anger bubbled up more and more as time passed by. I had started my life of faith in God, but when the passion I had begun with started to cool down, nettles of hatred began to shoot up in my mind.

Also, as I experienced the nepotism and secret deals that occurred behind closed doors in the Korean legal system during my divorce suit as well as through the incident with the homeless people, I became disgusted with Korean society's corruption, hedonistic values, and immoral culture. Seeing my ex-husband, the people around him, or the sheer immorality in society, I felt that nothing could ease my anger unless fire fell from the sky, completely burning up the odiousness.

Grace had flickered out in a single moment. Instead, a fire of hatred blazed within me as I began to build up the frameworks of the law, criticising others and committing murder in my heart. However, through my life in the wilderness situated in the small British isle, God allowed me to walk closer to Him, step by step, as time passed.

CHAPTER 10

A Waiting Rose

As soon as I saw the name, I took an instant liking to it. In Chelsea, there was a supermarket called Waitrose. When I had travelled to England on vacation, I usually bought food exclusively from Selfridges or Marks and Spencer. Beginning my new life in England, I shopped at Harrods' food hall or places around Ritz Hotel, an area with which I was familiar. But then as time went by, I became curious about the surrounding neighbourhoods and started to venture out to other supermarkets.

Only a corner away from my residence, boutiques like Chanel and Cartier lined the road. Harrods was be a farther walk away, towards the centre of London. Harvey Nichols stood on the opposite side.

King's Road, however, started out from the right of Sloane Avenue. Waitrose stood a few minutes' walk down that road.

When I first saw the sign, I wondered what a "waiting rose" could possibly be, but when I entered the shop, I found that it was a supermarket that wasn't as large as Tesco or Sainsbury's. Waitrose sold products of better quality.

When I first went grocery shopping, I didn't know the exact amount of supplies I needed or how to use them, so I had to ask the workers or other shoppers around me. Young people either shrugged their shoulders or talked so quickly that I couldn't understand what they were saying.

The old women, however, answered me kindly and explained things I didn't even think to ask about.

Before I put something in my trolley, I would scrutinise it for a ridiculously long time. If a box was slightly dented or the packaging was crumpled, I would dig into the shelves until I found one that was pristine enough for my liking. Now that I think about it, I feel very sorry for the employees who stacked the shelves after my shopping trips.

Also, I hated eating bread or biscuits that were squashed or deformed in the slightest. As if I were selecting a fine piece of artwork, I chose my confectionaries with the utmost care. Selecting each and every item in this way naturally meant that I literally spent hours shopping for groceries.

There was yet another reason why shopping took so long. It was the yellow sticker that I found on a few of the boxes. I saw these yellow stickers plastered on fresh groceries like fruit or vegetables, but I didn't realise what they were. I later learned that they were discount stickers. I assumed that sometimes when the worker was busy, only some of the products were discounted because the worker hadn't finished putting stickers on all of them. So whenever I went to buy groceries, I took a sticker and put it on the item that was the freshest, and then I put the item in my cart.

The people around me saw me groaning and struggling to peel of the stickers, but as no one said anything about it, it took me some time to realise what those yellow stickers were.

The elderly women in England have a way of smiling and greeting strangers. They always gave off a feeling of warm tenderness when I was around them. Even when I made mistakes and asked questions, they were very understanding and nice about it. If I was stumbling around by myself, not knowing what to do, they approached me carefully and explained everything clearly yet affectionately, as if they were talking to their own daughter. Sometimes they would be very talkative and treat me as though I were family although they had only just met me.

One day, I had been frustrated taking off the stickers and was grumbling to an old woman next to me, saying, "I wonder if the workers here ever finish something they start." As mentioned before, I later realised that the yellow stickers were selectively placed on the products that were close to the expiry date. Until then, I had been taking off the stickers and putting them on fresh groceries, thinking that the workers hadn't bothered sticking them on all the items.

When I realised this, I felt extremely sorry to Waitrose. I had been buying fresh goods at discounted prices. I saw how the British were fair and conscientious even when it came to business. They lowered prices of food that only had a few days to go. After I understood this, I promptly stopped peeling off the stickers.

When seeking out yellow stickers, one of the lessons I learned while living in England was frugality. As frugality is one of the Christian virtues, and as patience is a characteristic that the Bible names as an essential fruit of spiritual maturity, I received the teaching that I urgently needed. From January 1995 to February 1998, I was still paying for the divorce suit and had no source of income whatsoever. Having given up all my assets during the divorce settlement, I barely had any money left by the time I arrived in England. When I exchanged all I had into pounds, the little that remained shrunk almost to nothing. Today, the value of the pound has depreciated significantly, standing at about eighteen hundred Korean won. Back in 1998, however, Korea had been hit with the IMF crisis, so a single pound was equivalent to roughly three thousand won. After I had rented out a small flat to stay in and paid for basic living expenses, I found that twenty thousand pounds disappeared before I knew it.

When I went to buy glue for my daughter's school homework, I found that it cost one pound for a single stick. "How can glue be thirty-five hundred won? In Korea, it costs five hundred!"

In 1998, the pound seemed very expensive. As I converted pounds into won, I fell into a state of panic. I thought that I would eventually stop converting the price to won each time I went to the shops, but these frustrating calculations continued until the day I left for home. When I got home in 2006, I was stunned to see the exchange rate for the pound. One pound amounted to only two thousand won. I had been living eight years in England since 1998, after the Asian IMF crisis, when the dollar and the pound were at their peak.

Frantically, I was forced to cut costs. From our studio in Chelsea, my daughter and I moved around London, looking for the most affordable accommodation. For years, I rarely bought new clothes. Children's books were a luxury saved for birthdays and Christmases for my daughter, who loved to read. As for the glue, I made it from scratch out of flour, which worked surprisingly well. Thrown head first into a livelihood of yellow tags and reduced prices, I started to learn the value of money and the value for cost.

In this sense, my life in England was like frugality training. Being thrifty, not only economical, and wisely managing one's possessions is part of the Christian mindset.

CHAPTER 11

Learning Patience

I am inherently an extremely impatient person. If there is anything delaying me from buying a product I want or finding out something I'm curious about, I almost go mad with frustration. I can't watch TV dramas because I always have to know what happens next. When I read a book, I finish it in one sitting. Unable to wait for anyone or anything, I didn't even stand in queues back in my early days in England. I preferred simply to leave the shop.

Not being able to wait wasn't even half the story. If someone didn't follow my orders immediately, I would get angry. I even raged at people who talked slowly, as I was unable to bear the frustration. This was the reason I tended to avoid people in general, except my parents and the workers at my old house. I grew tired of having to swallow my impatience, gritting my teeth, and faking a smile. Human interaction was tiring and more than frustrating—so I tried to evade it as much as I could. As a result, I spent much of my life in withdrawal, living in my own world.

Fluctuating on a scale ranging from explosive impatience to utter meekness, I painted a smile on my lips every day. This was me. Even after I read the Bible through God's grace, it took me many years to overcome my bad temper and habits.

A Waltz of Grace

London transportation is infamous for its breakdowns and delays. While Koreans were mounting up their cattle, the British were boarding trains. Railways in England have more than a hundred years of history, so unless new lines are laid down, most trains and railroads are rundown and inevitably break down from time to time. Every day, I struggled with this broken system in order to get to my daughter's school on time to pick her up after my own classes at the university had ended.

At each delay or breakdown, I tried to be patient, but the mental picture of my child waiting at the school gates with her teacher put me at my wits' end. Whenever the train stopped or was delayed even by a few minutes, I felt like I was about to explode in frustration. This became such a bother that I ended up hiring a pickup woman to look after my daughter until I arrived to take her home.

Trains weren't the only problem. Everything about life in England was slow; nothing was done on the spot. The British seemed to spend half their lives waiting in a queue. In Korea, whether you are hiring a plumber or at an office, if you put in a request, it gets submitted and the work gets done that very day. Businesses in England, on the other hand, seemed to be closed half the time, on "bank holidays" or some other eventful day. When they were open, it took about a fortnight for something to get done, and that was if you were lucky enough not to go through a month-long delay.

There was a countless number of times when I felt as though I were imploding with frustration. But when I looked at the English people sitting alongside me, I saw that waiting was habitual. These people were not just respectable; they had the patience of saints.

Even if the train suddenly stopped on its way, no one would utter a word but would remain sitting quietly without any complaint. Waiting quietly was something that was obvious to the English. Once the train had been standing for twenty minutes and I couldn't sit still any longer. I jumped up from my seat and raged, "Stupid! Stupid country!" as I stormed down the aisle. However, not a single person even looked up to identify the person who had stood up to pace the aisle. I was the one who was surprised by the people who continued to sit silently, minding their own business. Suddenly, I felt very embarrassed. There I was, in someone else's country, rampaging about with no manners. After that incident, I sat silently, too.

Then one snowy day, the train came to a stop again. As usual, the people in the carriage sat, waiting without a word or absentmindedly biting on their nails. It was so silent in the train right then that it seemed like a world without sound. Finding myself in sync with this new world, I sat through the twenty minutes and looked out the window, unflinching and without making a sound. There was a curious harmony between the silence in the train and the sight of the fields outside steadily becoming covered in snow. Instead of leaping up from my seat in anger, I began to compose a poem:

> Raynes Park mounting up in snow
> The trees that wear clothes of white
> A silent landscape
> The people in the train sit still
> Not even a breath is heard
> As if stepping into a time machine
> That is being sucked into another world
> The British who sit so still
> In the land of ice that is their own
> Have no use for the fire in me.

CHAPTER 12

The Dose of Love, Mercy, and Grace

During the divorce suit, I had given up all hopes of reclaiming my assets. But a while after I had blown away everything I had through my "act of mercy," reality came like a punch to the gut in the form of my monthly bank statements. As my overall balance began to dwindle, the decreasing figures started to magnify before my eyes.

Regrets started hitting me like rocks. I wondered if I had done the right thing by letting C. take all I had so thoughtlessly, so recklessly. I had even handed over a market stall I owned at the biggest market in Seoul to get my daughter back under my custody.

When the unexpected divorce had come, I sought after God. No matter what life threw at me, my faith could not be shaken, as the world looked brighter through the eyes of grace and thankfulness for salvation. Every single day, my heart was filled with thanks and songs of praise. However, after going through the divorce settlement that dried me up financially, my human nature once again began to stir. Hatred rose up within me. I started to dwell in feelings of regret and remorse, which grew stronger and stronger each day.

"That evil man! How long are You going to let these sinners get away with what they've done?" I said to God.

All I wanted to know was when my ex-husband would pay for all he had done. As for his family, his friends, and the people around him, I regarded them as filthy, corrupt lowlifes. At the time, I was sick and tired of living in Korea, a country that had failed to show justice. I raged at God like Jonah longing for the destruction of Nineveh.

My parting words to my ex-husband at the divorce trails, "Believe in God and be saved before you die," now seemed completely inane and ridiculous. Even though God had granted me a brand new life, saving me from living an empty, pointless drudgery of bondage, I fell back into the swamp of resentment and hatred that pooled up in my mind.

I soon forgot my first love for God and began complaining like the Israelites in the wilderness. Even though I had seen God's hand work mighty wonders and His arm of salvation, this all evaporated from my mind. I was, yet again, rolling in the ditch of resentment and hatred.

I was like the merciless servant who had been forgiven his debts by his master yet put his fellow worker in prison for not paying him back. I hadn't been able to forgive my ex-husband and had lost the grace of salvation. When you are trapped in a dark pit of loathing and seem unable to forgive a person, your spiritual vision dims and you cannot see God. If you can't see God, you start to lose His grace and, therefore, the peace in your heart starts to disappear. Hating a brother is the same as locking yourself in a cell. The one you imprison is not the enemy that you hate but yourself. That is why hatred and resentment are ultimately worse for you than for your enemy. God, wishing for the freedom of our souls, told us therefore to love our enemies.

> "Anyone who claims to be in the light but hates his brother is still in the darkness" (1 John 2:9).

> "And now these three remain: faith, hope and love. But the greatest of these is love" (1 Corinthians 13:13).

I prayed to God with a truly contrite heart. I repented for having hated my brother and not genuinely forgiven him even though I had received the grace of God, who loves and saves even misfits like me.

God wants His people to live in love. The essence of the instructions that God delivered to Moses on the stone tablets was that we should love Him and our neighbours. Jesus Christ fulfilled this command through the love of the cross, thus fulfilling God's set of laws. As Christians, we must follow Jesus' footsteps and become practitioners of love. This is certainly easy to say but difficult to achieve. As unfeasible as it may seem, it is not impossible.

If we truly love and revere God, then we must extend our love to our enemies. We cannot love and revere the invisible God when we can't even love those who are visible to our eyes.

Loving one's enemies is feasible if one is within God's grace. When we think of Jesus, who uttered not a word of resentment through his suffering, we see that there is not a single person whom we cannot forgive.

> "If anyone says, 'I love God,' yet hates his brother, he is a liar. For anyone who does not love his brother, whom he has seen, cannot love God, whom he has not seen. And he has given us this command: Whoever loves God must also love his brother" (1 John 4:20–21).

God is love. The physical form of this love, Jesus Christ, gave us the new law to love and become an example to others as practitioners of love.

> "My command is this: Love each other as I have loved you" (John 15:12).

> "A new command I give you: Love one another. As I have loved you, so you must love one another. By this all men will know that you are my disciples, if you love one another" (John 13:34–35).

Jesus' command for us to love God and our neighbours embodies all the laws. Unlike the Ten Commandments, this is not a law that regulates actions or behaviour but a law at a whole new level, a law that exercises control over even the sins of the mind and heart. Jesus said that "to hate your brother is murder and to envy others is stealing." Moses' code of laws had the framework of Jesus' law and regulated visible sin, but Jesus, who brought with Him the new law of love, taught that a person should be born again, completely refreshed from the heart.

All people are siblings and neighbours before God. God wants us to love each other and live out our lives in liberty. Loving God and our neighbours means forgiving those who have caused us grief and pain, praying for them to be blessed. This, ultimately, is a way of freeing our souls.

God's first commandment is for us to have no idols before Him. However, having the right relationship with God depends on how we love our neighbours. First, God puts us at peace with Him and then brings us to love our neighbours. In this way, He leads us to live selflessly, putting our egos to death. When people sin, they live only for themselves and deal with others based on deceit and in alignment with their self-serving purposes. For those who know God, however, the order of love is completely reversed. This is to say that a person acts according to his thoughts and state of mind.

Those who love their brothers from the heart are people who fulfil the law. "Whoever has my commands and obeys them, he is the one who loves me. He who loves me will be loved by my Father, and I too will love him and show myself to him" (John 14:21).

Those who offer their lives to Jesus through loving their brothers and sisters from their heart have already received the blessings of the kingdom of heaven.

CHAPTER 13

A London University

The English-language foundation course at a London university allows students to select classes from major courses. When I first started the course, my IELTS score was 6.0, which was above average back then. I received a mark of "merit" for my midterm exams. However, a young woman called R. from Algeria had been awarded with "distinction" and a diploma to enter undergraduate school. I ended the course holding only the certificate of completion.

I loved every minute of studying at a prestigious university that had produced globally renowned scientists. There was a chapel and a courtyard on the campus. Near the school of music, there were practice rooms, too. Every once in a while, I would go to the practice rooms to eat my sandwich and play the piano.

Those were the happiest days of my life in England.

The classes I took were science, grammar, and law. All three courses fascinated me. The professors were extremely intelligent. During literature class, I read Shakespeare's sonnets and learned about English compositions. In science class, I explored various themes in great detail. In one class, we students went to see an open human anatomy exhibition held at Elizabeth Hall near campus.

I enjoyed all of my subjects and was able to earn good marks easily enough, that is, with the exception of law. Not only was the course material challenging, but also the instructor, N., was a tough teacher. A no-nonsense woman from the north, N. was extremely strict and banned students from entering the classroom after ten minutes of tardiness. On the days I had N.'s class in the first period, I awoke feeling nervous.

To get to campus, it took me an hour's journey on the train and a bus. No matter how early I got out of my house, I would certainly be late if the train was delayed or the workers went on strike.

One day, I was rushing out of the house when I hurt my head. I was bleeding, but I ran to class as fast as I could, without even receiving the proper emergency care. I was little more than ten minutes late. N. had locked the doors after ten minutes, so I stood at the door knocking until she came out. I showed her my head injury and pleaded with her to let me into the classroom. She flatly refused. Despite the mitigating circumstance of my bleeding head, I was late, so I couldn't come in.

Most of the students in N.'s law course were English and majoring in law. As for me, I had struggled enough studying piano—there was no way I could catch up with the law students, no matter how hard I tried. I had to get good marks in every subject to gain a diploma, but this law course was a barrier on my path. The coursework was an essay comparing the law of one's home country with British law. In order to complete the coursework, I would have to read through related media content as well as six books for reference. Finishing all these tasks by the due date would be a race against time.

For about a month, I spent sleepless nights reading and filling myself up with hamburgers from McDonald's. After handing in my essay, I became sick from fatigue.

Whether I was occupied with studying or playing the piano, my daughter was always reading her book nearby. One day, I was studying when I heard my daughter crying. Alarmed, I asked her why she was crying. She answered that she was hungry. The sun had already set, but I hadn't even fed my daughter. I reprimanded her, asking why she hadn't told me she was hungry. She responded by saying that she didn't want to disturb me when I was studying. This was the kind of effort I put into studying. In the end, however, I didn't get the marks that I had wanted.

When I finished my English-language course, I could select a subject for my major. At that point, I wanted to study theology. In order to study theology, a minimum score of 7.0 on the IELTS is required. I retook the examinations several times, but I didn't score over a 6.5, this after studying strenuously for a whole year. Frustration overtook me. All the students from Algeria had started with a 5.0, but by the time they finished the course, they had earned a score of 7.5 or 8.0. I had retaken the exam multiple times but could only reach 6.5.

I couldn't meet the application requirements, so I decided to take the advice of a chaplain at the university and submit an essay on which I had received a good mark instead of relying on the IELTS score. However, once the results came out, I learned that I hadn't been accepted. Disappointed, I had no choice but to apply to other schools.

CHAPTER 14

The Pen Incident

Growing up, I noticed that my parents gave huge offerings to their church, but they were just as generous in their treatment of the pastors, supporting a great number of them, including the head pastor. Although I did not regularly go to church, I had seen the grand contributions my parents made, which led me to think that pastors were usually showered with expensive gifts ranging from suits and cash vouchers to health-care services, even.

During my high school years, my bedroom was on the ground floor, as were the kitchen, the living room, and the maids' room. My sisters and parents had their rooms upstairs on the second floor. Whenever we had guests, the guests would have to pass through my room or come in to take a look around my room on their way to the living room.

Although most of them have passed away now, pastors from my parents' church, along with some famous pastors, would frequently come to our house to dine and worship.

I didn't particularly like pastors at the time, but with my parents treating them like royalty, I got the impression that they automatically deserved the utmost service and best treatment.

Korean churches were too rowdy. I could understand that everyone had different preferences and ways of self-expression, but I couldn't get used to the banging beat of the drums or the way people sang loudly and boisterously during worship. Hearing them telling me to get up and dance was even more repulsive. I liked sitting quietly during service, in deep contemplation and listening to the choir sing Gregorian chants or anthems in Renaissance and early Baroque styles. Still, most of the churches in Korea had worship styles that were completely different from what I preferred.

English churches, on the other hand, weren't so noisy. They were mostly full of elderly people, and the services were quiet. I could feel that the worshippers had reverence for God through their hymns. Also, they looked truly humble with their hushed, quiet order of service.

I cried many times during St. G. Church's service. I couldn't help the tears, which would just pour down. When the service was over, the elderly women would pat my shoulders warmly, no questions asked.

Anne, from Scotland, was a female minister who had been inaugurated at the church after she finished her studies at one of the Ivy League colleges in America. One day, I invited her to my house. She came, and we talked about many things. I also started attending Bible study for women. While living in Chelsea, I had been bored without a piano at home, but I was allowed to practise on the piano at church. So that was what I did from time to time during the week. However, I couldn't attend that church for very long.

While taking the English course at the London university for a year, I had resolved to stay in England for a longer time. That meant I needed all my belongings from Korea. Since properties were too expensive in Chelsea, I decided I would move to the southern part of London.

After my lease ended, I started searching for a place to stay until I went back to Korea. I came across D. Hotel. It was only a three-star hotel, but the exterior looked neat and the rooms looked decent enough to live in for a month. But then yet another incident broke out.

I lost my most treasured fountain pen. It was a pen made by Cartier, a luxury item so beautiful that no other fountain pen could ever come close in comparison. It was work of art—sapphires were studded on the top and bottom, and the cap, made of 18 karat gold, bore panther spots.

It was a pen that took my breath away. Once, at St. G Church, I lent it for a moment to a woman with cropped hair and glasses who needed a pen. Upon seeing it, she gasped and said, "Wow!" The pen drew the eyes of everyone who saw it. It was a limited-edition, handmade product.

It was that very pen I had lost, and I was devastated. I couldn't afford to buy a new one. Even if I had the money, it would be impossible to find another. For several days, I cried, thinking, "God hates my having the things I love."

Then, one of the mums from my daughter's nursery school heard my story and advised me to report it to the police. Desperately hoping I could find my beloved pen, I went to the police station and filled out a report for theft. I explained my story in great detail, even drawing the policemen a picture of the pen. Then, after a few days, the inspector in charge told me he would start an investigation. I had been suspicious of E., the hotel manager where I was staying.

As the hotel room was scruffy, I had tried to brighten things up by decorating the space with the luxury items I carried around with me. I put the fountain pen on the side table and placed a Cartier ink bottle next to it. Then I stacked up gift boxes under it.

Whenever I travelled, I prepared small presents that I took around with me. They were mostly small, light items like ginseng tea or candies that I would give to show thanks or when I felt like I was short of tips. These things were always in the same place. I knew exactly where everything was.

Thinking through the situation over and over, I could only conclude that a person with the master key had taken my fountain pen. I tried to think of the person who would have the master key. Either the manager or the cleaning lady was the likely culprit. Then, one day, the middle-aged cleaning lady told me that E. liked fountain pens.

With the weight of the crime falling on E., I started interrogating her. Scoffing, she scathingly asked me why a person with such an expensive pen would stay at that hotel. Treating me with contempt, she accused me of telling lies.

It was the last Sunday before I was to go back to Korea. I was telling a couple of people at the church about the fountain pen incident and asked one of them, a short-haired woman, if she remembered my pen. She shrugged her shoulders, obviously not caring, and told me she didn't remember it at all.

As I looked at her with a blank expression, a wave of emotions flooded over me. Right before the fountain pen incident, I had gone to Chanel to buy several bottles of Cristalle to give to this short-haired woman and an elderly woman who had always been kind to me in church. I felt hurt, wondering if the woman had misunderstood my show of thanks as putting on some sort of show. I was convinced that the short-haired woman remembered my pen. But then she seemed to be looking at me with an air of distrust. I cried that night, too.

It is the same way in Korea now, but in England, the police would go everywhere in pairs. Also, their walk was different from ordinary people's. Whenever I spotted policemen near me, I always felt happy to see them, feeling as if they were escorting me.

English policemen are sharp. When they are going through investigations, they don't miss a single detail. The *007* series isn't a story made of fluff. Through the theft of my pen, I became aware of this fact. If I had had the receipt from purchasing the pen, then I could have made a claim to my insurance company. However, there was no way I would have thought of such a thing, as I was unprepared at all times.

I had bought the pen from Cartier's main store on Rue St.-Honoré in Paris, but I had no means of proving this. There was a way of asking for reparation for lost property abroad if I submitted the receipt of purchase and filled out a form reporting the loss. However, I didn't have the essential documentation with me and couldn't prove that I had ever possessed the pen.

I wanted the police to launch an immediate investigation into E., the manager of the hotel, and get my pen back. I had thought that if the short-haired woman would bear witness that I had once owned the pen, then this would be enough evidence to launch an investigation into E. However, the short-haired woman had brushed away this opportunity with a single sentence. The disappointment that I felt lasted until I returned from Korea, ridding me of any desire I had to go back to St. G. Church.

CHAPTER 15

Anne

All the ministers in England were extremely humble-hearted. I felt that their lives of faith were very pure. Their sermons were simple but had profound meaning that moved my heart. Compared to the pastors of Korea's megachurches, the simple lives of these English ministers were humble and modest. Seeing them, the image of Jesus in his ragged clothing arose in my mind, once again filling my heart with emotion.

I met Anne on the Sunday before I returned to Korea. As a token of thanks, I wrote her a check for three hundred pounds so that she could go out for lunch with the other ministers at St. G. She told me she couldn't accept it. I insisted that she take the check. Finally, she relented and told me she would give it to the church. I thought of the pastors who would boldly ask my father for huge sums of money in offerings. Thinking of the contrast between Anne and them, I was moved once again.

The head minister made an announcement after the service on that last Sunday. He said that they were collecting money for a charity but were yet short of a thousand pounds. I instantly wrote a check for a thousand pounds and gave it as an offering. That was my last Sunday at St. G. Church.

A couple of days before my flight, the police came to the hotel for investigation. After they had looked around my room from top to bottom, even going into the bathroom, they pointed at the boxes covered in gold gift wrap and asked me what they were. I explained to them about the present boxes.

Several days later, at the hotel reception desk, I picked up a letter from the police confirming the case of theft. Then I left for Korea as planned. Packing up my belongings in Seoul, I sent them to England before I went back and moved to another church.

A dramatic start to my life in England, this episode also marked the next chapter of my life of faith as I grew in discipline and learning. As I had been blessed by the melodic hymns of St. G., I began to serve as a pianist in the choir at my new church.

Also, through the philosophical and scientific viewpoint I had used in the past to criticise Christianity, my eyes finally opened to the presence of my Maker as I tirelessly perused books on science and philosophy, and even other religious texts, to understand my God. The rest of my life in England was a time of spiritual nourishment, my coming to understand the deep and mysterious providence of God.

PART FOUR

Seeing for the First Time

PART FOUR

Seeing for the First Time

During my eight or so years in England, I read countless books on science, philosophy, psychology, astronomy, and even biology to satisfy the curiosities I had always had about Christianity and God. I even read the religious texts of Buddhism, Hinduism, and Islam. To share my investigative study over the years, I would like to highlight a collection of findings and musings that have fascinated me in my quest to grow in knowledge of God.

CHAPTER 16

The Bible and Numbers

In high school, physics was one of my favourite subjects. Nothing excited me more than studying the laws and theories of physics along with mathematics. For me, maths and science were as logical as philosophy, as pure and as beautiful as music. I had fun lining up numbers and thinking about the laws of physics.

After I started university, I didn't have a chance to continue studying physics or maths. Despite having forgotten most of what I had learned in high school, I still enjoy reading about theories and playing around with numbers. Elementary maths keep me entertained for hours on end.

The Bible contains a lot of numbers—numbers of days, months, years, people, and so on. However, the numbers are not simply figures; they have symbolic meaning behind them. As I read the Bible, I started to see that all studies of the world are interrelated and that the acme of any field of study points to God.

There are many cases in which the laws of physics apply to psychology and the human mind. For instance, the law of inertia can be applied to people with inactive personalities or to their psychological tendency to try to be satisfied with their circumstances.

$1 + 1 = 2$
$1 + 2 + 1 = 2^2$
$1 + 3 + 3 + 1 = 2^3$
$1 + 4 + 6 + 4 + 1 = 2^4$

1
1 1
1 2 1
1 3 3 1
1 4 6 4 1

$11 = 11^1$
$121 = 11^2$
$1331 = 11^3$
$14641 = 11^4$

$\pi = 3.14159265358979...$
$3^2 \times 4^2 \times 5^2 = 3600$

$1 + 2 + 3 = 6$
$1 \times 2 \times 3 = 6$

$1 \times 2 \times 3 \times 4 = 24$

$1\,4\,2\,8\,5\,7 \times 7 = 999{,}999$

$\infty = 0$

9
9
9

1 Absolute number; absolute God; $1n = 1$
2 Number of witnesses; disciples sent out in pairs
3 Holy Trinity; the number of heaven
4 Number of the world; four creatures; four ends of the earth
5 Number of grace; Pentecost
6 Number of the fall; number of the beast
7 Number of completeness; day of rest
8 Number of resurrections
9 Characteristics of the fruit of the Spirit
10 Number of the abundance of the world
12 12 disciples; 12 tribes; 12 crowns; 12 stars
24 24 elders; 24 treasures (signifying the members of the church)
40 years of training: Moses' years of training in the wilderness; the fasting of Jesus
666 Number of the beast; number of judgement
144,000 People from the Old and New Testament who are saved

CHAPTER 17

The Circumcision of the Mind

When solving sets in mathematics, you find that the more empty sets there are, the total number of sets expand accordingly, as empty sets are subsets of sets containing elements. In this way, "circumcising" the mind means to expand one's capacity of reasoning unlimitedly, which should be done objectively without any prejudice or preconceptions.

When you're walking the path of life, you will come across various types of people and all sorts of situations. A person who lives life without trying to understand others, stubbornly refusing to break out of his or her conventional views of self-righteousness and prejudice, has a mind that is uncircumcised.

However, those with open attitudes who try to understand others have minds that have been circumcised. Since the Middle Ages, Christianity has been perceived by some as a religion of self-righteousness and narrow-mindedness. Religious leaders claiming to believe in God ignorantly handled developments in science or astronomy, which gave people the wrong perception of God.

Theories of biology, anthropology, evolution, and other things that could be comprehended in various different ways were flatly rejected and suppressed with the claim that they did not fit into the religious framework of Christianity. When there are issues that anthropology, biology, science, or any other field of study cannot resolve, we should not continue to engage in never-ending debates with other people. Instead, we should seek the answer in the Word of God.

All theories and claims must be processed with a more open mind. As there is a working "room" for various converging studies, such as physics and mathematics, the Bible, being extremely vast and dealing with the dimension of a higher Deity, certainly has enough "room" to embody all areas of study in the world. The modern person living in the twenty-first century has seen the evolution of science as well as human intelligence reaching a level that is almost incomparable to that of the nineteenth century. However, the giant leap that people of the future will make with the development of quantum mechanics will be unimaginably great.

As science progresses more and more, our perspectives should broaden accordingly. Within the space of a three-dimensional world, a single fact can only ever be a mere fragment of the whole truth. Within hyperspace, it may not even be a truth on its own. Partial truths can always come into conflict with each other, but they all may be a portion of something that is true in another dimension.

The facts, or truths, that we know from anthropology, biology, or the theory of evolution are only fractions of the whole truth. However, human beings, each armed with different partial truths, argue with each other viciously, insisting that they are right while discounting the views of others.

However, Christians should try to understand with a more open mind and an attitude trusting in God. He is complete, whereas our human understanding cannot soundly judge or be certain of anything. When God created the world, He gave humankind the authority to rule all creation on earth, but through the act of sin, humans have rather degenerated to a position where they are being ruled by the earth.

God desires for humans to be recreated as truly universal people. In demonstration of this, the Israelite nation practised circumcision as a mark of being a chosen people. In the same way that God distinguished

Israel as His chosen nation, we, as the spiritual Israelite people did, must live bearing the circumcision of the mind. "A man is not a Jew if he is only one outwardly, nor is circumcision merely outward and physical" (Romans 2:28).

CHAPTER 18

A Made-Up God?

> In his pride the wicked does not seek him; in all his thoughts there is no room for God.
>
> —Psalm 10:4

We are undoubtedly living in the most globalised generation in all of history. A single word uttered in one part of the world can cause a huge commotion in another. The words of influential people have the power to move others on an international scale.

Prejudice is something that is universally held by every human being. While it may channel some outward influence, it can have a particularly powerful impact depending on who the person is.

Just because a person is an eminent scholar does not mean he or she knows God. There are many cases in which one's intelligence rather acts as a stumbling block, causing one to stand against God. A person is no more than a speck on the surface of the earth, a ball which isn't even visible as a speck in our solar system, which in turn is a mere dot within the vast universe. Yet people shrink God down to their own size and speak of Him unintelligibly.

Despite the peak age of science and the apogee of human intelligence, the primitive question about the existence of a god has continued to be debated through time. Putting forward universalism, determinism, or some other ontological theory, theists argue for the existence of a god against atheists, who reveal their own foolishness by attempting to refute matters of spiritual concern using materialistic evidence.

Because atheists try to understand issues of the spirit and mind in the context of the visible, material world, the arguments they offer are futile and a waste of time. Also, whether one may be an atheist or a theist, all human knowledge is incomplete in every aspect. The Bible holds all the answers, but there is not yet anyone who understands it fully. Although there may be some who claim to know it all, they are in fact spiritually deaf. An argument with these atheists is a folly from the very start.

Richard Dawkins claims there is no God. It appears that he is confusing religion with God, which is his very first mistake. Religion was not created by God but was formed by people. A person who refuses to accept God because He cannot be explained theoretically or made visible to the human eye is ultimately blind in the mind. To open the eyes of the mind, one must take off the peel covering them. This peel is the hard covering of a strong ego that is full of ignorance, prejudice, and self-righteousness. This shell must be cracked and the mind made humble in order for the eyes of the mind to open wide.

People have the tendency to make judgements according to their knowledge or experience. However, even if a person possessed all the knowledge in the world, there is a limit to how much a human being can ever know. Even if the top scholar or specialist of a certain field, a person cannot know absolutely everything about the world. Humans are quick to judge and draw conclusions in situations that they cannot understand through their own knowledge or experience.

Using this tactic, the evil spirit that denies and twists the existence of God has been on the move since the beginning of human history. That is why it is important for the human soul to get to know the Bible by way of more through, dedicated meditation. After reading the Bible from cover to cover, one simply cannot say that God is a "delusion."

God is not some genie that can be imagined and made up by people, and He does not disappear or cease to exist even if people deny Him. Those who deny the existence of God are people who live empty lives and do not know their own purpose or the value of their own existence. They are hollow, confused people. Speeding towards death, they are unable to see in the total darkness they have willed upon themselves. In that sense, atheists are the most pitiful beings in the world.

God revealed Jesus through the language of humankind. Throughout the history of Israel, He manifested Himself and explained His existence to people. He is a being who exists on His own terms—by Himself and through Himself. When He appeared to Moses, He described Himself as being "Who I am."

Meanwhile, a delusional, made-up god refers to idols crafted by humans. Those who make up gods are people who idolise themselves, power, titles, or money.

When those who call themselves intelligent people or geniuses deny God and twist facts about Him, calling Him a made-up "delusion," other people who are unfamiliar with the Bible can easily be led to confusion.

This is especially the case when an internationally eminent scholar claims that God is a cruel, sadistic deity. Those with weak faith or non-believers may wonder if the famous scholar is right and dubiously agree. For instance, in Genesis 3, it is clear that Eve, in the garden of Eden, didn't have the conviction of faith and held the wrong information about God.

In reality, intelligence is not a force against God but a tool needed to understand Him, who is great and almighty. It is actually through reason that one's spirit can grow in depth. All throughout human history, God has constantly revealed Himself. He wants people to have firmly grounded knowledge of who He is.

> Ask now about the former days, long before your time, from the day God created man on the earth; ask from one end of the heavens to the other. Has anything so great as this ever happened, or has anything like it ever been heard of? Has

> any other people heard the voice of God speaking out of fire, as you have, and lived? Has any god ever tried to take for himself one nation out of another nation, by testings, by miraculous signs and wonders, by war, by a mighty hand and an outstretched arm, or by great and awesome deeds, like all the things the LORD your God did for you in Egypt before your very eyes? You were shown these things so that you might know that the LORD is God; besides him there is no other. (Deuteronomy 4:32–35)

> Acknowledge and take to heart this day that the LORD is God in heaven above and on the earth below. There is no other. Keep his decrees and commands, which I am giving you today, so that it may go well with you and your children after you and that you may live long in the land the LORD your God gives you for all time. (Deuteronomy 4:39–40)

It is the will of the one and only God of heaven and earth to enrich us with blessings and eternal life. He does not degrade or devalue us, although He would be justified in doing so. Earnestly, He calls out to us today, urging us not to choose the curse of being separated from Him through disbelief but to take eternal life the very moment that the good news falls upon our ears. The reason God has people walk a path through the wilderness is to bless them and give them eternal life.

> "He gave you manna to eat in the desert, something your fathers had never known, to humble and to test you so that in the end it might go well with you" (Deuteronomy 8:16).

> "And now, O Israel, what does the LORD your God ask of you but to fear the LORD your God, to walk in all his ways, to love him, to serve the LORD your God with

all your heart and with all your soul, and to observe the LORD's commands and decrees that I am giving you today for your own good" (Deuteronomy 10:12–13)?

His command to and rule for us is twofold: to love Him and to love our neighbours. This command seems difficult to keep, given the fallen human nature, but if God gives us His grace, it is not impossible.

> Now what I am commanding you today is not too difficult for you or beyond your reach. It is not up in heaven, so that you have to ask, "Who will ascend into heaven to get it and proclaim it to us so we may obey it?" Nor is it beyond the sea, so that you have to ask, "Who will cross the sea to get it and proclaim it to us so we may obey it?" No, the word is very near you; it is in your mouth and in your heart so you may obey it. (Deuteronomy 30:11–14)

To be able to keep God's commands, we must keep close to His Words and also testify to and manifest His truth with our minds and lips. God, whose mercy is unlimited, desires that even Richard Dawkins should come to repentance and receive salvation. Even if Dawkins doesn't know God, God certainly knows him. Not only does God know Dawkins, but also He loves and cherishes the souls of all non-believers who do not know Him.

In the book of Jonah, God told the prophet to go to Nineveh in the Kingdom of Assyria and spread His Words there, warning them of impending destruction. He did not destroy them with a curse as He had prophesied once. Everyone, from the king to the common peasant, listened to Jonah and repented with humble hearts. "When God saw what they did and how they turned from their evil ways, he had compassion and did not bring upon them the destruction he had threatened" (Jonah 3:10).

God, who knows every soul even before it is born into the world, is the actual form of love. He waits for the very last person on earth to return to Him in repentance. Therefore, all non-believers must not delay but must return to God once they hear the good news. Even now, He is calling out to them and waiting for them to come back to Him. "Seek the Lord while he may be found; call on him while he is near. Let the wicked forsake their ways and the unrighteous their thoughts. Let them turn to the Lord, and he will have mercy on them, and to our God, for he will freely pardon" (Isaiah 55:6–7).

CHAPTER 19

The Name of Religion

Needless to say, there are many different religions in the world. Each religion's adherents have their own particular title for their subject of worship, or god. However, there is only one true God. God is not confined within the frameworks of what we call religion. Religion and God are undoubtedly separate. God is a spiritual existence without form, and religion is phenomenon of systematic order built up by humans.

God is not a physical existence like us humans with faces and features. Many have attempted to create images of God or have even tried to materialise solid forms of Him, yet He is not truly present in any of those forms. That is why the Bible says that those who worship Him must do so in truth and in spirit. "God is spirit, and his worshipers must worship in the Spirit and in truth" (John 4:24).

Although humans live in a materialistic world, they are able to sense the supernatural and spiritual world to a certain extent. Even beliefs such as totemism and animism can explain the basic spiritual nature of a person.

God is indeed a mysterious entity. The human response or reaction to His existence is manifested through religious activities. That is why religious communities are formed and distinctive beliefs systematically take shape, according to the surrounding environment and cultural norms, and eventually become defined as a form of religion.

Most of the time, however, people easily mistake religion for the character of God Himself. That is why humans clash with each other, even going to war, and families fall apart—all in the name of religion. Despite people's "holy" justifications of them, these situations have nothing to do with the will of God.

Also, God is not a god of war who delights in conflicts and bloodshed, unlike what Richard Dawkins claims. God is the form of love itself, and the Bible manifests this truth. God is pleased when people love each other and live practising His mercy and love in kindness, rather than fight each other within the framework of "religion." The history of humankind is within God's work of extensive salvation. In order to fulfil the work of redemption, He chose the Israelites as His people and, through them, revealed His existence and His righteousness to humankind. "'Am I only a God nearby,' declares the Lord, 'and not a God far away? Who can hide in secret places so that I cannot see them?' declares the Lord. 'Do not I fill heaven and earth?' declares the Lord" (Jeremiah 23:23–24).

God reveals His existence through natural creation so that people can feel their way to discovering Him. He intends for us to realise that He is always close to us, never far behind (Acts 17:27). Therefore, people cannot give the excuse that they do not know of the existence of God. "For since the creation of the world God's invisible qualities—his eternal power and divine nature—have been clearly seen, being understood from what has been made, so that people are without excuse" (Romans 1:20). That is why the countless forms of religion or non-biblical practices made by humans are all useless, seeing as God is the one true form of religion. Therefore, the important thing is to understand the true form of God and put this knowledge above any religious ethics or practice.

God used the Bible as a channel of proclaiming His love for and salvation of humankind through Jesus Christ. With Jesus' name's having been clearly proclaimed, we humans must turn back from stumbling down the path of ignorance and fix our eyes on Him. People's fighting each other in the name of religion is by no means what God ultimately wants. Violent conflicts "in the name of God" are strictly attributable to the lunacy of religious groups or radicalism—they are irrelevant to God Himself.

He who sent His Son into this world to die for humankind is the God of love. Even today, He is working through the Holy Spirit and pleading on the behalf of ignorant humans in inexpressible groans. However, when we look at history, we see many repetitions of incidents in which the name of God has been twisted in the name of Christianity. Confining God under the name of Christianity is grievously wrong. It is possible for Christianity to exist as a religion under God, but it cannot, in any way, overshadow Him. The countless mistakes caused by Christianity through generational misinterpretations and the misjudgements of a number of religious leaders have clouded the true image of God and all His glory. It must not be forgotten that God Himself is the very core of the Christian faith and that He works through His book, the Bible.

In conclusion, God is not constrained within the religious framework of Christianity. However, God does work through Christianity because He revealed Himself through the Bible, which is the foundation of the Christian belief. In the past, He administered His works through the Israelite people, but in modern times, He continues to unfold His work of salvation through Christians, His spiritual people. Therefore, even in this world where many Christians go against the Words of God by living their lives in hypocrisy, people must fixate their eyes on God alone. Also, before pointing at the speck in our brothers' eyes, we must pull the planks from our own.

Although one should live with a strict, self-critical attitude towards oneself to make sure that he or she is not violating the Words of God, one must treat others with love and understanding at all times, living a life that gives glory to God.

CHAPTER 20

Christianity and Other Religions

With whom, then, will you compare God? To what image will you liken him?

—Isaiah 40:18

During my English studies at a London university, there was a time I was studying with a group of Muslim students from Algeria. These students were on a national scholarship given to eminent students who scored within the first fifth percentile on the International Baccalaureate, a test similar to the College Standardised Admission Test in Korea.

In addition to having their university fees waived, these Algerian students received full funding of their living expenses. I noticed that during Ramadan, they would spend almost a month not even drinking a drop of water. They all believed that they would become saved by keeping the Five Tenets of Islam and rigorously fasting throughout the Ramadan period.

One day, when I asked R., the cleverest of the Algerian students, if all the kids from Algeria "do the same thing," she replied that they did as if this was an obvious fact.

"Oh my goodness! I could never do that! How do you manage it?"

This exclamation had shot out of my mouth, totally in Korean. R. looked at me for some time with an expression of bewilderment. Feeling embarrassed, I said to her in English, "I really respect you all."

In stark contrast to these people who were living out diligent lives of faith despite having the wrong kind of teachings and beliefs, I had not often properly prayed or fasted, although I claimed to believe in the living God. Compared to their obedience and lives of faith, I seemed like a non-believer, far beneath their standards. Seeing them rigorously keep religious laws and practices that even orthodox Christians would find hard to follow gave me many things to think about.

I jumped at every chance to ask R. questions about how I should gain salvation of the soul. She answered me as best as she could, saying, "Allah, who can sense the difference in weight of a single feather, will weigh your actions in life. If you have done more good, you will go to heaven, and if you have even a little more of evil, you will go to hell."

I told her, "I don't doubt that the almighty Allah is the only one who knows the difference between grains of sand even, but if he sends people to heaven or hell based on that 0.00001 per cent of difference, then he is not a fair god."

It is all well and good for those who went to heaven by way of that tiny weight of difference, but for those who are receiving the punishment of hell, it is extremely unfair and unjust in the eyes of anyone. I asked R. another question.

"I've read the Qur'an out of curiosity, and it said, 'How can you not believe that a virgin can give birth? There is nothing Allah cannot do.' This means that Muhammad accepted the fact that Jesus was born through the Virgin Mary. But then, if he regarded Jesus as one of the many prophets, isn't this an inconsistent fallacy?"

If the words of the founder of Islam and the beliefs of contemporary Muslims are different, isn't this a fallacy? If you believe that Jesus was born through a virgin, then how can you place Muhammad, who was only human with Original Sin, above the Messiah Jesus?

I continued with my questions, "If the Qur'an is a completely accurate book containing the Bible, and if it accepts the contents of the Bible, then how can it possibly deny Jesus the Messiah, to whom the Bible essentially points, while claiming the law-based means of salvation through keeping the Five Tenets?"

R., later, looked at me with a serious expression on her face, telling me that she had never really thought twice about Islam before since she was born into the religious environment. Now that she had started thinking about it, she felt that she had a lot of questions and wanted to try reading the Bible for herself. When we graduated, I gave her an English Bible as a gift.

I earnestly prayed that the bright, kind, and pretty person R., and all the Algerian students I had studied with at the university, would come to the know the true God.

As I began to think about the salvation of souls and come across friends and acquaintances of different faith, I decided I should learn about other religions as well. I believed that if I wasn't aware of the illogical nature and errors of various types of non-believers, debating with them would only be futile and drag on forever.

That is why I perused everything I could regarding the origin of religion, the three major faiths, and the beliefs of Confucianism and Taoism. After reading various religious texts, I came to a conclusion that Christianity did, indeed, stand apart from other religions of the world.

I began with Buddhism, as it is the second largest religion in Korea. I learned that the founder of Buddhism, Siddhartha Gautama, who was born into a noble family, left his home to live a religious life of self-penance, but, in the end, he could not save his own soul. He lived a life of self-denial, lived to be older than the age of eighty, and was surrounded by loyal followers, but, in the end, he could not deny his own appetite and suddenly died of enteritis caused by overconsumption of food.

Jesus, who gave His own life to save the world in His thirties, only at the dawn of His life, is incomparably different from any other teacher or religious founder that ever existed, even when looking at Him from a humanistic perspective.

Siddhartha's teachings are philosophical and have many aspects that we may learn from on a humanistic level. However, he could not provide a clear answer to the question of saving a human soul. Through self-penance, he claimed to have attained enlightenment, but he was referring to death. Also, his books hold no evidence of his being saved and gaining eternal life.

As for Hinduism, I read the Upanishads, the sacred Hindu text, and discovered a number of contradictions. The claim that humans are within an eternal cycle of life but are able to break out of it through enlightenment of the truth is very similar to a claim of Buddhism. However, no answer can be found in the Upanishads, either.

Only if Hindus and Buddhists substituted the "realisation of truth" with the Word of God would they have something approximating the right idea. However, as they do not accept the Messiah or the Words of Jesus, they will continue in their cycle of karma and samsara, with no means of escape.

Philosophy, Confucianism, and the words of Lao-tzu and Chuang-tzu are only humanistic schools of thought. While they can provide some food for thought in philosophical reasoning, none of them can give an answer to the question of salvation.

Humans cannot save themselves. Even if a person were to live a life dedicated to attaining enlightenment, he or she could not enter into true enlightenment while in the body of a sinner without first clearing up his or her Original Sin. Also, no matter what kind of ritual one may follow or how much one may suffer through self-penance, such efforts cannot rid the mind of sin. If good deeds or self-penance could gain somebody salvation, then Jesus' blood on the cross would have been utterly meaningless and unnecessary. "I do not set aside the grace of God, for if righteousness could be gained through the law, Christ died for nothing" (Galatians 2:21)!

We can only be saved through believing wholly in Jesus' grace and His able hand, by which He first offered us the token of salvation. Siddhartha Gautama is not the Messiah. He was an ordinary human being who simply attempted to find the whole truth through suffering.

In the Old Testament law, there is a rule: "Where there is sin, there is death." If there is sin, then death must follow; and just because a person is 0.00001 per cent a sinner, he or she is not different from those who are 99.999 per cent sinners. If we apply the true-or-false proposition to this situation, then we see that a saint and a malicious criminal are both sinners when they stand before He who looks into a person's heart.

The Ten Commandments are specific to the laws of the body, but the command given through the love of Jesus' cross is a law of a much higher degree. According to this law, which regards avarice as the same as having already stolen and regards hating a brother as equivalent to murder, there is not one person on earth who has dutifully kept it.

Only Jesus Christ, who came through the history of the universe without Original Sin, is a Man of completeness. The rest of humanity are sinners. Therefore, in this catch-22 situation where sinners can do nothing but die, God set forth the law called love, but without compromising His complete justice.

He turned Jesus Christ into a living sacrifice, as Christ satisfied the requirement of an offering that was complete in an impeccable body free of sin. Jesus Christ's life that was given on the cross for the sins of humankind was a pleasing sacrifice that satisfied the impartial judgement of God. There is no other way of salvation than this.

Considering the nature of religion, in that it pursues "good," the various types of religion may appear similar on the surface. But when it comes to the issue of human sin, there simply is no religion other than Christianity that is complete and just, offering a clear solution and a scenario in which God unilaterally reaches out to humans and completes the salvation of the soul through the death of atonement. Through the Words of the Bible, God proclaimed His message of salvation to people on earth. No other religion on earth speaks of a God who came into a specific space and within a specific time frame of history to save humankind, bearing the body of a man and dying hanging on the cross, bearing the punishment in the place of sinners.

Christianity is a religion based on the Bible. The core message of the text proclaims that a person can be saved by faith through the faultless, precious redemptive blood of Jesus, who was fully God but at the same time born completely human. This salvific message simply cannot be discovered in any other religion—and it is ultimately the Word of the only God.

CHAPTER 21

Is Christianity Self-Righteous? Discovering Faith

One of the reasons why I didn't go to church as a child, despite my father's forceful insistence, was that Christians seemed extremely self-righteous. All religions looked roughly the same in that they pursue goodness, but it annoyed me to no end when Christians insisted that they were right and all others were wrong.

When I saw pastors or churchgoers force religion on others, telling them they should "just believe" without offering any logical evidence for having such faith, they sounded amazingly stupid to my ears. I decided that these unintelligent people who couldn't tell their right from their left were making absurd claims to others through blind faith.

In those days, I thought that any intelligent person should know the works of ancient Greek philosophers like Plato, and philosophers from the Middle Ages as well as those from more contemporary times, such as Kant, Hegel, and Descartes, in addition to psychology, in order to be considered capable of holding a decent conversation.

I also thought that logical reasoning required mathematic knowledge through the study of Pythagoras, Euclid, Gauss, Riemann, and Einstein. That was why I would snub anyone who spoke without a foundation of what I considered to be rudimentary knowledge.

The written works of great thinkers were like teachers and friends that influenced most of my early life. However, the philosophy books I read with such fervour couldn't provide me with the answers to my questions about the meaning of life or eternity.

There are innumerable books in the world. From ancient to contemporary times, texts have inspired and captivated the hearts of countless thousands of people. Each text has its own merits. However, no book has been read or loved as much as the Bible. The Bible is the Word of God, and it has the power to transform people. It is also a timeless book that amazes by reaching out to each and every person in a different way. Its Words work uniquely in each person, whether he or she is completely uneducated or has the highest education and utmost knowledge.

Some say that the more you know, the harder it is to have faith. However, high intelligence paves the way for deep spiritual understanding. The Bible stirs emotion in people according to the length and width of their reasoning. Such emotions are unique to each individual and incomprehensible by any other. That is why I see the Bible as a book that holds many dimensions within its covers.

When I went through my divorce, a time of trial in my life that I could not understand, I turned to the Bible. I started reading Exodus where the pages fell once I flipped the book open. Then, as I read more and more, passage after passage, I became so absorbed that I finished reading the entire Bible in a week, from Genesis to Revelation.

In case there were parts that I had misunderstood because I had read too quickly, I read the Bible again, for a second time, but carefully switching between the Korean and English versions for reference.

Then, I read through it again, comparing it with biblical commentaries of William Barclay and Dr. Yoon Sun Park that were sitting in my father's bookshelf.

I was amazed. It came as a shock that the Bible wasn't the childish, fictional story that I had heard during those times I had been dragged to church, but that it was the Words of the living God.

After that point, my values and beliefs were turned completely upside down. I started going to church even though no one was shoving me into the car. The God I had met was not self-righteous at all. He was a merciful, graceful God who had brought about incredible works by allowing humankind the free will to love Him in return.

The more a person comes to know the Bible, the more humble, faithful, and upright he or she will become. As Jesus' disciple, a person will realise the importance of understanding other human beings and will love them all the more.

In this way, the Bible is a book that is a positive force for transformation. After I read the Bible, my entire life started to change. Even my temper and bad habits began to dissolve. From a wandering life swayed by useless wants and desires, my life had been transformed to one that had a clear purpose for being. This life is one that compensates for the grace that I received, one that sets my sight upon God's main focus, which is the saving of souls.

When the Word is being spread, people must open up their hearts and accept it in faith. The Bible uses the word *today* to refer to a present state of receiving the good news. It means to tell us that we must receive this news when we hear His voice today, without any obstinacy (see Psalm 95:7–8 and Hebrews 3:7).

Receiving His voice, His good news, we must let go of our obstinate minds and replace them with repentant ones. At the gate of God's kingdom, we mustn't stand there awkwardly; instead, we must walk the narrow road along with Jesus in order to reach the final destination. Believing in the good news of Jesus is an act of faith that opens the door. If we walk to the end, abiding with Jesus, then we reach completeness in our faith.

Depending on the person, there are countless dimensions of faith. Paul's definition of faith is twofold. The first I refer to is Romans 1:17, which reads, "For in the gospel the righteousness of God is revealed—a righteousness that is by faith from first to last, just as it is written: 'The righteous will live by faith.'"

Here, Paul categorises faith into two types: faith of the beginning and faith of the end. Faith of the beginning refers to the first step of faith, in which a person hears the message of salvation and opens the doors of the mind. The second part, "living by faith," refers to a firm, resolute faith that will not stumble in any situation.

Then, how must a person completely believe and trust in God? The answer is the Bible. God reveals His personal information through the Bible. That is why it is crucial for us to listen to His Words. As Paul also said, "Consequently, faith comes from hearing the message, and the message is heard through the word about Christ" (Romans 10:17).

A person who lives every day listening to the Words of Jesus Christ and meditating upon them will become a person of complete faith who fully experiences God in his or her mind and life.

A person with completeness in faith is a person who knows God fully as if talking face-to-face with Him. This type of individual cannot be shaken, owing to his or her conviction of salvation.

God made humans so that they would give Him praise. Thus, this is our ultimate purpose in life. "The people I formed for myself that they may proclaim my praise" (Isaiah 43:21). Also consider this: "For now we see only a reflection as in a mirror; then we shall see face to face. Now I know in part; then I shall know fully, even as I am fully known" (1 Corinthians 13:12).

Abraham, the father of faith, started his journey from Ur of Chaldea. "He went out, not knowing" where he was heading. Despite this uncertainty of direction and destination, Abraham, through his complete faith, became the progenitor of faith for all generations to come. His life is not so different from the lives of ordinary believers today. He was a person of great faith who had left Ur of Chaldea but hovered in the middle, at Haran. Wherever he went, he lied without certainty of faith and chose to bear his first son, Ishmael, through human methods.

However, with the confirmation of his belief at Mt. Moriah, Abraham became a person of wholesome faith whose heart was one with God's. He came to believe that God was the Almighty One with the authority and power of resurrection to raise the dead from the ground.

This teaches us the practical life of faith that produces the fruit of Jesus' true love. That is why Christians, as the disciples of Jesus, must live exemplary lives that practises the two great commandments of loving

God and one's neighbours. "A new command I give you: Love one another. As I have loved you, so you must love one another. By this everyone will know that you are my disciples, if you love one another" (John 13:34–35).

Jesus came to the world in a lowly, humble form and gave His life for humankind. If Christians do not live by the example of Christ, then they can only become stumbling blocks for non-believers, hindering them from taking a step of faith. The wrong image of Christians can only cloud up the glory of God. This serves as the primary reason why Christians, as saints, must live holy lives each day.

The most common dilemma for Christians is today is their double life of faith. They claim that they are believers but do not really know very much about the Bible. This is a serious problem. Lacking knowledge of the Bible, they live the same lives as non-believers and are just as vulnerable to the lures of sin, but, with the claim that they "believe," they cause others around them to become tempted.

Prodigals who leave their father's house and get themselves into trouble still have the chance to return home (Luke 15). However, the seemingly good sons who stayed home all along can be just as misguided. Their self-righteousness and arrogance covers up the mercy and glory of their Father's forgiveness, grace and glory.

Non-believers have the hope of repenting and returning to God, but the hypocrisy and misdeeds of Christians can only be a hindrance to the salvation of souls.

Throughout history, there have been many cases where supposed believers of God have caused Christianity to become misinterpreted as self-righteous by their failing to live exemplary lives of faith and misusing the Bible to justify their actions. However, God Himself is not self-righteous, and there is no other salvation but the one He gave us through the good news of Jesus' cross. "Salvation is found in no one else, for there is no other name under heaven given to mankind by which we must be saved" (Acts 4:12).

In conclusion, Christianity based on the Bible is not self-righteous. Self-righteous are the corrupt Christians who mislead others by their hypocritical actions, but God Himself is not self-righteous at all.

CHAPTER 22

The Mind of God

However, if we discover a complete theory, it should in time be understandable by everyone, not just by a few scientists. Then we shall all, philosophers, scientists and just ordinary people, be able to take part in the discussion of the question of why it is that we and the universe exist. If we find the answer to that, it would be the ultimate triumph of human reason—for then we should know the mind of God.[1]

—Stephen Hawking

When reading the works of Steven Hawking or Michio Kaku, you will discover that not only are these scholars pre-eminent in their fields of research, but, based on their rather philosophical words, they are also religious. The issue of God's existence is inevitably brought up when the subjects of human nature and the creation of the world are discussed.

Within history, humans have only recently made several steps to significant discoveries. Even so, human beings are different from other animals in our level of ability to reason. Human beings have been expanding their reason while asking universal questions about the nature of humankind and the purpose of existence.

Michio Kaku says in his work *Hyperspace* that the mere fact that humans have an understanding of scientific reason despite their finite abilities of thinking in itself makes life worth living.[2]

Some people seek the meaning of life in personal achievements, relationships, or life experiences. However, being blessed with the capacity to know the secrets of nature has enough meaning in a person's life. To put this in religious terms of a repentant Christian's confession, we can translate: "The true meaning and purpose of life is more than enough when praising God and having a heart that knows Him."

Behind each theory of physics is a mathematical explanation that automatically backs it up. This is also the case as regards philosophical propositions. Ultimately, all fields of study are linked to religion. We now explain this as the concept of convergence. We humans, who have been like apes as far as standards of rationality go, have now reached a point in time where we must evolve to a level where we can distinguish God's heart based on the insight of the universe. In which direction is God's heart pointing? His sight is decisively set on the people on earth. God wants all humans to gain salvation.

Who will live according to God's will once realising the intentions of His heart? It is the people who know God. If a person does not know God, then he or she cannot know what is in His heart. In the Bible, God's state of mind and desires are revealed.

After becoming more knowledgeable about the Bible, I prayed that I would live a life according to God's purpose for me but it took me a long time to realise what this was. What God desired wasn't some grand, dramatic mission but simply for me to believe in His words and live a life in faith.

When a person starts a life of faith, he or she must break out of elementary faith and reach a level of maturity so as to distinguish good from evil. This is how a person can make God happy—by acting in goodness and not losing out to sin. As with mature adults who are considerate of their parents, we must become people with mature faith in order to understand the mind of God and to know what makes Him happy.

In His mind, God craves for the salvation of the human soul. He wants every single person on earth to gain eternal life and wishes that people would understand His state of mind. He desires to give people hope and peace in their lives. "'For I know the plans I have for you,' declares the Lord, 'plans to prosper you and not to harm you, plans to give you hope and a future'" (Jeremiah 29:11).

What God intends for His people is for them to have peace and hope. He wants them to receive the blessing of being joyful and living in peace. God's invitation of love is open to all people and discriminates against no one.

Many atheists claim that that the God of Christianity is a cruel, racist deity of war who shows favouritism, preselecting those who are saved and those who are not. However, that is completely false. God is the true form of love. If a person were simply to repent, then He is merciful. "Now reform your ways and your actions and obey the Lord your God. Then the Lord will relent and not bring the disaster he has pronounced against you" (Jeremiah 26:13).

The very heart of God desires for all people to be saved.

> "Do not repay evil with evil or insult with insult. On the contrary, repay evil with blessing, because to this you were called so that you may inherit a blessing" (1 Peter 3:9).

> "God our Saviour ... wants all people to be saved and to come to a knowledge of the truth" (1 Timothy 2:4).

The cross of Jesus Christ is a door to salvation that is open for all humans. This door of salvation is open for anyone to enter. Also, God is love. "For God so loved the world that he gave his one and only Son, that whoever believes in him shall not perish but have eternal life" (John 3:16).

God's will for us in Jesus Christ is that we always walk the path of goodness. The heart and intention of God regarding humankind is for people to live lives that don't repay evil for evil but that pursue goodness instead. The good news brought through Jesus' cross ultimately delivers the highest dimension of love, which suffers for others. This is what God's heart and mind are aimed at.

This conclusively means that it weren't a specific, hand-picked people that God exclusively selected, He selected goodness nevertheless. He has chosen goodness while discarding evil. He wants humans to choose goodness, too, and thus receive eternal life.

An example of this can be seen in Genesis, which dedicates many chapters to the well-known story of Jacob and Esau.

The two brothers Esau and Jacob were fighting while within the womb, each wanting to get out first. The prelude of this story illustrates that although there is an ongoing battle between good and evil inside every person's heart, evil comes out first, every time.

Jacob was a historical figure, the tribal leader of Israel, but he is also representative of a selfish, opportunistic manipulator. Esau signifies the fallen people who have exchanged God's Word for the world through their materialistic greed.

The concept that we call predetermination does not indicate that God makes a discriminatory selection of humans to salve. People are sinners with a humanistic nature that always produces evil first. However, with the healing of His Word, goodness soon follows. In the order of good and evil, evil is illustrated as the firstborn son, whereas the second-born signifies good that has been reborn through the Words of God.

The Israelites, as the physical firstborn, were the chosen people of God, but when Jesus Christ was given over to be nailed on the cross, the exclusive Word of God passed over to the foreign nations. This is why all foreigners who believe in the good news of God have become His chosen people through His spiritual appointment. The firstborn Israelites are the physical descendants of God whom He has deserted; second-rate foreigners have taken their place. This is why the concepts of "firstborn" and "second-born" are not simply literal but imply a spiritual meaning.

Although evil presides first in a soul that has sinned, if that soul is tamed through God's Words, then good will flow out of it. Such work of transforming evil into good is the creation of heaven and earth expressed in Genesis. There probably is not a single person who believes that the history of the world spans only six thousand years. Although species such as *Anthropoidea* and *Homo sapiens* were early "humans," those who were reborn as true humans made in God's image had ethical intelligence. God created *Homo ethicalis* to be able to understand logic and language with God's intelligence and also make decisions using God's wisdom. At least this is my hypothesis.

The literal interpretation of the Bible is important, but as the Bible is sealed by the locks of parables and symbols, it must be read in great detail in order to know its true meaning.

> Then I saw in the right hand of him who sat on the throne a scroll with writing on both sides and sealed with seven seals. And I saw a mighty angel proclaiming in a loud voice, "Who is worthy to break the seals and open the scroll?" But no one in heaven or on earth or under the earth could open the scroll or even look inside it. I wept and wept because no one was found who was worthy to open the scroll or look inside. Then one of the elders said to me, "Do not weep! See, the Lion of the tribe of Judah, the Root of David, has triumphed. He is able to open the scroll and its seven seals." (Revelation 5:1–5)

The words of the sealed book are the Bible, and the seven sayings of Jesus upon the cross are the seven seals in Revelation. In the same way Jesus moved the hearts of His disciples when He abided with them on the road to Emmaus and interpreted the Bible with various parables, He stirs up our hearts also and presents us with the Holy Spirit as a gift. Also, like it says in Paul's sermon, we are living in the generation of grace, in which the Bible is made clear to us as if we were looking at Christ face-to-face.

That is why we must hold the Words of God in our hearts and get to know Him completely. We must be born again as people who live complete lives.

> "Do not merely listen to the word, and so deceive yourselves. Do what it says" (James 1:22).

> "In your relationships with one another, have the same mindset as Christ Jesus" (Philippians 2:5).

CHAPTER 23

On Happiness

Happiness depends upon ourselves.

—Aristotle

Human happiness cannot be discovered in material objects but within the mind. Marcus Aurelius claimed that happiness was showing goodness to others, whereas Pascal said it was disabusing oneself of obsessions. Schopenhauer said that happiness comes from a peaceful mind, and Kant said it was a state of comfort and satisfaction of the mind. Tolstoy said that happiness is within our hands. Other great thinkers, like Emerson, Spinoza, Hegel, Seneca, and Voltaire, all attempted to define happiness, but compared to the Bible, their knowledge is incomplete.

The Bible immaculately clarifies the term *happiness,* about which humans know only vaguely. The happiness of life ultimately comes down to knowing God, practising His purpose-filled love, and praising Him in our lives. Within this kind of life, there is a source of infinite happiness that the world cannot ever offer.

What kind of person receives blessings from God? It is a person who reveres God, puts hope in Him, and chooses to be helped by Him.

> "Blessed is the people of whom this is true; blessed is the people whose God is the Lord" (Psalm 144:15).

> "Blessed are those whose help is the God of Jacob, whose hope is in the Lord their God" (Psalm 146:5).

God focuses on people who choose and seek Him; in this, He plans to bless them. If a person decides to follow God, keeping far from sin and living in goodness, then he or she becomes a person who is blessed. Those who choose disbelief instead are cursed. The will of God is to save humans through the cross of Jesus Christ, and this cross signifies the love of One who suffers and gives up His own life for others.

Happiness is about sharing with others (Acts 20:35), living out God's Words (Jacob 1:25), being peaceful with others (Matthew 5:9), upholding justice by living righteously (Psalm 106:3), and being patient through faith until the very end (James 5:11).

Then, who exactly are blessed people? The Bible defines them in the following way:

> Blessed is the one who does not walk in step with the wicked or stand in the way that sinners take or sit in the company of mockers, but whose delight is in the law of the Lord, and who meditates on his law day and night. That person is like a tree planted by streams of water, which yields its fruit in season and whose leaf does not wither—whatever they do prospers. (Psalm 1:1–3)

A blessed person is someone who always meditates on the Bible, trusting in it and living in thankfulness through joy. Happiness is not far away. Many great thinkers such as Tolstoy have said the very same thing.

It is true. Happiness is always near and upon our lips, with which we can sing. It is also within our hearts and has the ability to allow us to be joyful during sad times.

CHAPTER 24

The Three Temptations of Humankind

Regardless of the person or the situation, people face three types of temptations in life.

Before Jesus started His public life, He fasted for forty days in prayer. When He had finished praying, the Devil tempted Him, who was then in a state of extreme hunger, "If you are truly the son of God, then turn this rock into bread."

Satan derisively struck Jesus with the temptation of turning a rock into bread when He was exhausted from weeks of starvation. In this way, Satan shamelessly awaits the chance to tempt us when we are weak.

Esau is a biblical figure who lost out to the weakness of the body. Unable to withstand even a day of hunger, he exchanged his rights of a firstborn to satisfy his stomach, thus becoming the model of foolishness and irrationality.

The sheer hunger Jesus felt must have been inexpressible in words after His fasting for not just a couple of days but forty. However, He passed His first test by quoting words of Deuteronomy: "Man does not live by bread alone, but by every word that comes from the mouth of God."

"Then the devil took him to the holy city and had him stand on the highest point of the temple" (Matthew 4:5), the Bible says.

With the words, "Do not test the Lord your God," Jesus cast away the second test.

Then, "The devil took him to a very high mountain and showed him all the kingdoms of the world and their splendour" (Matthew 4:8).

At this point, Jesus said, "Away from me, Satan! For it is written: 'Worship the Lord your God, and serve him,'" gaining victory in the third test as well. The three temptations directed at Jesus are the rudimentary tests of the sinful cravings of a human being, the lust of his or her eyes and the boasting of what he or she has and does.

The first object of temptation for people in the likeness of God's image which led to their downfall was the fruit in the garden of Eden. This fruit was extremely desirable to the woman in that it looked very appealing, delicious, and enlightening, but God had strictly forbidden Adam and Eve to eat it. "Do not love the world or anything in the world. If anyone loves the world, love for the Father is not in them" (1 John 2:15).

Pursuing the desires of the body, selling oneself short for a piece of bread, filling up the lust of the eyes through vanity, becoming secularised by chasing trophies in this life—all of these ultimately lead to destruction. Eve, who didn't have full knowledge of God's words or a sturdy belief in Him, ended up losing out to the temptation of the Serpent, but Jesus Christ, who was the symbol of the second Adam, completely defeated Satan with words from Deuteronomy.

If Jesus Christ, the human form of God Himself as well as the Lord of all creation, humbly used the words of the Bible to overcome the temptation of the world, then we, too, can surely be victorious in the very same way. We cannot win over the temptations of the world with only our morality or our own righteousness. If a person is self-confident in believing that he or she is morally impeccable and has values firm enough to resist evil temptations, then he or she lives with a humanistic misunderstanding and a serious case of arrogance.

We cannot overcome Satan's temptations with our strength alone. We must be armed with the right beliefs from the Bible and with firm faith in God to win against a world that is full of temptations. Jesus accepted the authority of the Bible as the Words of God, giving reference to it as He relinquished Satan's enticement—and this is shown as an example to all people.

There are three main categories of temptations, although they come in different forms depending on the person. In order to stand firm against Satan, who prowls like a crying lion, trying to make believers stumble in faith, we must meditate upon God's Words each day and lean on them in everything we do.

CHAPTER 25

When Eve Saw the Tree

> When the woman saw that the fruit of the tree was good for food and pleasing to the eye, and also desirable for gaining wisdom, she took some and ate it. She also gave some to her husband, who was with her, and he ate it too.
>
> —Genesis 3:6

People tend to make judgements based on what they see. Erich Fromm, a social philosopher, wrote that in the "cup" of our motives, ideas, or beliefs, there are various kinds of false information and prejudice, irrational emotions, and preconceptions mixed inside. The small pieces of truth that drift atop the mixture deceive people by making them believe that the cup contains the whole truth. Like Fromm's analogy, there are countless cases in this world where the truth is manipulated and swallowed up by lies. The fallibility of human judgement easily produces such errors.

Each person has his or her own way of looking at the world. In the garden of Eden, Eve heard the words of God through Adam, but she didn't have firm faith in them. That was why she couldn't give a definite answer based on God's words to the Serpent, who questioned her using various facts in a dubious manner. She answered him uncertainly based on her thoughts, even adding words of her own.

The moment that the Serpent heard the woman's answer, which was lacking in knowledge as well as certainty, it seized its opportunity. Telling Eve that she "surely will not die," he knocked down her faith in one blow and succeeded at tempting her.

Adam, who had heard the commandment directly from God, did not firmly plant it into the woman's mind. The woman didn't know very much about the commandment and didn't fully believe in it, either. So when she listened to the words of the Serpent and looked at the tree again through worldly values, she suddenly saw that the fruit looked good to eat and was pleasing to the eye, as well as desirable in that it would give her knowledge. The sinful cravings of humankind, the lust of the eyes, and the boasting or the pride of life captivated her in that single moment.

That was why the woman "stretched out her hand" and took the fruit. When the mind is filled with desire, a person acts on it accordingly. The woman who had eaten the fruit gave it to Adam also. Adam didn't even ask what it was; he ate it without much thought. There is much meaning in this scenario. God didn't call out to the one who had sinned initially, but He called out to Adam first. "Adam, where are you?" God asked.

This wasn't a question asking Adam where he was physically, like a game of hide-and-seek, but it was the heartbroken voice of God questioning the ontological status of humanity. Hiding because of his shame, Adam had degenerated from ruling God's creation to being ruled by it instead. Instead of repenting, he started justifying himself and blamed the woman in words marked with accusation against God.

After posing the ontological question to Adam, God turned to the woman, asking her the reason for her actions. The woman, in turn, transferred the blame onto the Serpent.

God did not even bother questioning the Serpent. He directly cursed it and condemned it, as it was the very form of evil. It received the daunting judgement of having its head crushed by the Messiah, Son of a woman. God said to the Serpent, "And I will put enmity between you and the woman, and between your offspring and hers; he [Jesus] will crush your head, and you will strike his heel" (Genesis 3:15).

The Serpent's head's being crushed signifies the death of Satan. From the very beginning, God proclaimed this destruction of evil. The snake biting the ankle refers to the way Satan attacks the weak points of human beings, similar to the story of Achilles' heel in Greek mythology.

Satan never ceases to bite at our weaknesses and make us stumble into temptation. In my case, I have fallen over many times because of my impatient temper. When you fall over, you can hurt yourself, but there is also a possibility of death. That is why Satan incessantly roams around like a crying lion, looking for prey to devour. "Be alert and of sober mind. Your enemy the devil prowls around like a roaring lion looking for someone to devour" (1 Peter 5:8). This is why we must always be awake and on full alert. When looking at the story from a physical perspective, it may seem as if the Serpent's words were true, seeing as Adam and Eve did not die immediately after eating the fruit, but this is not the case.

Adam and Eve were physically alive, but their souls had perished the very moment they sinned. Separated from God and having lost their original place in existence, they were hiding, huddling in the darkness as they shook in fear. God sought them out first, asking Adam where he was. While we were still sinners, God came to find us first. Sinners do not go looking for God on their own accord. The grace of God that seeks out humans first is what we call the good news, or the gospel. It is the Word of God.

The Serpent is a realist and is a symbol of evil pursuing hedonism and physical comfort. This realist Serpent, who is the Father of Lies, succeeded in making the woman sin by lying to her confidently, saying that she would "surely not die." Again, Adam's and Eve's bodies did not physically die. However, God's perspective considers the soul.

Spiritually speaking, Adam's and Eve's souls had already left God and died the very moment they ate the fruit and sinned. The state of having a dead soul means that a person is void of life, although his or her body may be alive.

The Bible likens hedonistic people who sin for momentary pleasure to those who are dead. "But the widow who lives for pleasure is dead even while she lives" (1 Timothy 5:6).

In reality, God did not immediately put sinful humans to death. Humans who have sinned will have not a single trace of them left once they die physically.

The same was true in Noah's situation. Although it was Ham who found Noah lying naked and drunk from wine, it was Ham's son Canaan, whom Noah had cursed. When reading Genesis 9, one comes to wonder why Canaan had to receive a curse for his father's sin.

God treasures humans with His heart. However, He is intolerant when it comes to sin. Ham was in the wrong, but his body did not die immediately. The attributes of sin inside him were symbolised by his son Canaan, which was later the name of a nation filled with wrongdoing and sin.

This case follows the same logic as Genesis 3.

After Adam and Eve were forced to leave the garden, God clothed them in clothes made of leather. As the leather must have been acquired through the shedding of an animal's blood, this signifies the generations that would live under the law. Regulating human behaviour through the law was a form of physically training humans until they put their minds straight and learned to control them.

Such physical training is essential, but it is even more important that one does not sin in the mind. When the mind is made new and a person reaches God's complete holiness and attains a life of firm faith, his or her physical actions, too, automatically become complete.

We are not fighting a battle of blood and flesh (Ephesians 6:12). If it were literally a physical conflict, then why would Jesus have had to bear the cross when He could have just come to the earth with lightning, thunder, or the armies of heaven and swept humans off the face of the planet?

The Enemy we are fighting is not a human being. Because of this, God doesn't want humans to start turning on each other.

Thus, our battle is not a physical one visible to the eye, but a spiritual war waged against the evil in this world. In order to win this war, we must put on the full armour of God and completely prepare ourselves with the shield of faith and the sword of God's Word.

> Therefore put on the full armour of God, so that when the day of evil comes, you may be able to stand your ground, and after you have done everything, to stand. Stand firm then, with the belt of truth buckled around your waist, with the breastplate of righteousness in place, and with your feet fitted with the readiness that comes from the gospel of peace. In addition to all this, take up the shield of faith, with which you can extinguish all the flaming arrows of the evil one. Take the helmet of salvation and the sword of the Spirit, which is the word of God. (Ephesians 6:11–17)

The Word of God, or the Bible, is the ultimate sword of God. In the midst of spiritual warfare, the sword of the Word is the greatest weapon given to us by God. "For the word of God is alive and active. Sharper than any double-edged sword, it penetrates even to dividing soul and spirit, joints and marrow; it judges the thoughts and attitudes of the heart. Nothing in all creation is hidden from God's sight. Everything is uncovered and laid bare before the eyes of Him to whom we must give account" (Hebrews 4:12–13).

People tend to fall into the pit of distraction, unaware that it is a trap, as they follow along the temptations of evil and are suddenly taken captive. In this way, the force of evil disguises its outward appearance in order to deceive the spiritually weak. The Bible says that Satan disguises himself as the angel of light. "For such people are false apostles, deceitful workers, masquerading as apostles of Christ. And no wonder, for Satan himself masquerades as an angel of light. It is not surprising, then, if his servants also masquerade as servants of righteousness. Their end will be what their actions deserve" (2 Corinthians 11:14–15).

However, Christians who stand upright in the Word of God are able to distinguish good and evil with the sword of truth so they are not so easily tricked by Satan's schemes. The force of evil started with the ancient Serpent and grew more and more evil, becoming a viper, which now leads people to the destruction of their souls by using all sorts of disguises. If the force of evil strengthens as we near the end of all time, then we must live lives that shine even brighter in goodness. We must also arm ourselves with the Word of God, who is complete.

We are fighting the aftermath of the war that already ended in Genesis, which is why we can surely be victorious, strengthened by the able blood of our Messiah, Jesus Christ.

CHAPTER 26

The Paradox of Life

> A man can see other people's shortcomings and vices, but he is blind to his own. This arrangement has one advantage: it turns other people into a kind of mirror, in which a man can see clearly everything that is vicious, faulty, ill-bred and loathsome in his own nature; only, it is generally the old story of the dog barking at its own image; it is himself that he sees and not another dog, as he fancies.
>
> —Arthur Schopenhauer

Life is full of paradoxes. Against good, there is evil. Without light, there is darkness. All natural phenomena in the world have a hidden side and an opposite force that contradicts them. In the same way, when people feel that they are inadequate for something, they try to cover up their weakness by wrapping themselves up. People live by decorating only the side of themselves that is visible to others.

Green glass appears green in the light, but—a surprising fact—it actually does not contain any wavelengths of green. This concept of "appearing as if something exists" can be applied to life, too. Schopenhauer said that while people cannot see their own evil and faults, they can instantly find them in other people. He also said that, in this way, humans display the tendency of a dog that barks at its own image in the mirror.

The dog barks aggressively at its own reflection, thinking it is another dog. Once you begin to see another person in a hateful way, you must realise that the other person is a reflection of yourself and strive to fix that part inside yourself first. You will realise: "The person I hate is the very image of me."

God told us not to hate anyone and to love even our enemies. The person whose characteristics I detest has been put in my life by God as a tool to fix my own weaknesses. When one starts to think in this way, then that detestable person no longer seems all that hateful. When God tells us to love our neighbours as we love ourselves, we ourselves are included in this love. That is why loving our neighbour is equal to loving ourselves in the end. After realising this, I started to gradually understand other people.

All humans have a sinful nature but many attempt to better themselves by clothing themselves in vanity. All humans, who were born with the Original Sin of Adam, are incomplete within their inner selves. However, it is a mistake to think that such hollowness can be filled with humanistic, earthly efforts. Even if a person were to be dressed exquisitely in authority, honour, or wealth, his or her inner vacuum could not be filled.

Only the Words of God can provide the solution for the emptiness that people feel. That is why the words of Deuteronomy, "Man shall not live by bread alone, but by every word that comes from the mouth of God," stand, unchanging in truth.

> Be careful to follow every command I am giving you today, so that you may live and increase and may enter and possess the land the Lord promised on oath to your ancestors. Remember how the Lord your God led

> you all the way in the wilderness these forty years, to humble and test you in order to know what was in your heart, whether or not you would keep his commands. He humbled you, causing you to hunger and then feeding you with manna, which neither you nor your ancestors had known, to teach you that man does not live on bread alone but on every word that comes from the mouth of the Lord. (Deuteronomy 8:1–3)

I always hated extremity of any sort. But then every part of my life has rocked back and forth, from one extreme to another. In everything, the most dramatic things have occurred. I had a foul, impatient temper, yet, at the same time, I had an indecisive personality that made me dither until I was shocked to my senses. I work harder than anyone, but then the rest of the time I would be completely lethargic. When I was burning with passion, I would spend a sleepless night tirelessly working on something until I finished it, but the rest of the time, I would do the bare minimum. In school, I earned top marks in the subjects I liked, but in the subjects I didn't care for, I was right at the bottom.

My lifestyle was reflected by my report cards. On one hand, I wanted to live a quiet life in retreat, but, being the way I was, I lived standing out from others, creating boisterous commotion as I lurched from one extreme end to another. I hated myself and my life.

However, with His Words, God came and found me in all my uselessness. From that point on, my life rapidly began to change into a more positive one. This amazing paradox cannot not be denied.

God takes pity on the empty, troubled human soul that wanders in the darkness. He created light in the world through His Words. God's Words to humankind are the light of salvation and possess the authority to raise the dead. A full day in Genesis starts with night, which morning follows. "It was night and then it was day."

However, in the human perspective, daylight comes first and then it is night. Genesis, written by Moses, describes the historical works of salvation by God, who chases out the darkness and evil in a person's soul with the light of His Words. Chapter 1 of John says that in the beginning, there was light. That Word was light revealed through salvation, and it was Jesus who was with God from the very beginning. "In the beginning was the Word, and the Word was with God, and the Word was God. He was with God in the beginning. Through him all things were made; without him nothing was made that has been made. In him was life, and that life was the light of all mankind" (John 1:1–4).

God created the entire history of redemption through His Word, which is the light of the people, is life itself, and is Christ. That is, people must take in God's Word just like the Israelite people in the wilderness filled themselves with manna in order to live. The Word of God is the food of life, and this supplement can save the soul.

The *Chicken Soup for the Soul* series has long been a bestseller all around the world. In the same way that soup is more smoothly swallowed than solid food when we are sick, comforting words are good for the mind when it is in pain. Whether the words are religious or not, words that relax a soul prescribe a cure called "emotion."

However, no matter how many books or inspirational words a person may read, the thirst of his or her soul doesn't dwindle. Good words or beliefs simply cannot save a soul or give life to it by any means.

Anyone who reads good books like *Chicken Soup for the Soul* becomes emotionally moved. However, if the person reads the book a couple of times, he or she finds it boring. The Bible, on the other hand, is food for the soul that tastes finer and finer the more you eat it.

Healthy people can't live by eating nothing but plain soup every day. They need proper meals that are filled with all sorts of nutrients. If healthy people lived drinking only soup every day, then they would soon become malnourished.

The only food that can save the soul is the Word of God. The Bible, as the Word of God, offers not only soup but also different types of vegetables, as well as a variety of filling food. It is a premium buffet that has tables stretching out with dishes of every kind of food imaginable. As there are many different kinds of food that are suited to individual tastes, the new believer can take in soothing words like soup while sturdier people can take in more solid food, words that require a higher level of understanding. The Bible is the Word of Life and makes each and every person healthy according to the condition of the soul. Also, not only is there food that helps a person grow, but there are also special dishes of the day containing words of grace.

The religious leaders in Jesus' day did not understand the Bible. Obsessively focusing on the laws, they lived lives that were conspicuously holy, but, on the inside, they had hearts as hideous and filthy as a dirty, crumbling grave. They were filled with hate, jealousy, pride, and greed. Although they recited the Bible day and night, they didn't understand what it was truly about. They acted like holy men on the outside, but their minds were filled with all sorts of unsightly sins. They babbled about serving God, but they were actually living lives that were far away from God.

Lust is more or less idolatry, but the Pharisees defined idolatry as bowing to a visible object of worship. So they believed they were keeping God's commandments by avoiding idols completely. However, Jesus firmly scolded them for ostentatiousness and misdeeds. He said, "Woe to you, teachers of the law and Pharisees, you hypocrites! You are like whitewashed tombs, which look beautiful on the outside but on the inside are full of the bones of the dead and everything unclean. In the same way, on the outside you appear to people as righteous but on the inside you are full of hypocrisy and wickedness" (Matthew 23:27–28).

The religious leaders did not recognise the Messiah, Jesus. Being filled with hatred and jealousy, they had crucified the body of God Himself, the Lord of all living things, accordingly to Roman law (Matthew 15:10). When Pilate was hesitant about issuing a verdict for Jesus' case, the Israelites said that their descendants would deal with the consequences.

Without proper knowledge of the Bible, we believers today are standing in the same position as the Israelites and Pharisees who had Jesus nailed to the cross—even if we go to church every day and night.

The Bible prophesies that Jesus, the Messiah, will return to the world. If we are to greet Him upon His return instead of nailing Him to the cross once again, we must know and understand the Bible. Upon our understanding, the hollowness of our inner selves, the confusion within, becomes subdued and we become able to reign over the darkness that embodies evil, such as hatred and jealousy. Then our lives will be overflowing with happiness and thanksgiving.

Those who live with thanks for and joy in all things are people who have rich, abundant souls. Those with abundant souls do not live a deficient life of poverty, hollow with the desires of the world; instead, the focus of their life is directed towards a positive light.

CHAPTER 27

Does the Bible Contain Errors?

Whether the Bible is reliable and the whole truth has been a topic of debate for the last few centuries. The argument continues to this day, after its confirmation as the legitimate text. It was at the Council of Jamnia around 90 AD when the thirty-nine chapters of the Old Testament, from Genesis to Malachi, were recognised as legitimate and when the New Testament of twenty-seven books, from Matthew to Revelation, was selected at the Council of Carthage in 397 AD.

Although there are many unofficial texts that exist apart from the sixty-six that were selected as the "Bible," these are only for reference. The essential points of Christianity are all laid out in the legitimate text. The apostle John said, "Jesus did many other things as well. If every one of them were written down, I suppose that even the whole world would not have room for the books that would be written" (John 21:25).

People who claim that the Bible has errors are those who take passages out of context and raise issues about them, judging the Scriptures with a scale of prejudice that they call knowledge and experience. I was one of those people. The Bible is a book of mysteries. Finding it difficult to understand is common to all people.

I'd always thought that my Muslim friend R., whom I met in England, would better understand the Bible than I if she were to read it with that clever head of hers. However, the heart of understanding also comes from God.

When I read the passage in Deuteronomy 29:4, "But to this day the Lord has not given you a mind that understands or eyes that see or ears that hear," I came to realise that the process of understanding the Bible is also under God's sovereign grace.

Ever since I was young, no matter how fun or interesting a book was, I would be sick of it after reading it more than five times. The Bible, however, grew more interesting, much more fascinating, the more I read it, once, twice, twenty times. The more I read of it, the more the verses I missed when reading it previous times would emerge, magnified and clarified. Each time I read it, a rush of emotion would come upon me as if I had discovered a chest of treasure.

This book that causes readers to discover a world of an upgraded dimension is an amazing book of possibilities. It is complete and without a single error for the following reasons.

First, the Bible itself holds the authority of God. Whether or not people may believe in it, it always has authority. It is the able Word of God that fulfils everything written in its pages.

> "God is not human, that he should lie, not a human being, that he should change his mind. Does he speak and then not act? Does he promise and not fulfil" (Numbers 23:19)?

> "So is my word that goes out from my mouth: It will not return to me empty, but will accomplish what I desire and achieve the purpose for which I sent it" (Isaiah 55:11).

The passages of Mark 7:13 and 12:36 show how Jesus Himself accepts the Bible as the Words of God recorded by authors who received inspiration from the Holy Spirit. What other evidence could we possibly need when all the prophets testified to God's Words and the Messiah Jesus approved of its legitimacy as the Words of God?

Then, the original question comes down to whether God in His completeness could make mistakes.

I, for one, strongly believe that there is no way God could have allowed any errors in the Bible.

Through our human eyes, it may appear as though the sixty-six books of the Bible were selected by religious conferences of the past, but those sixty-six books come down to the hands of God Himself, who moved the hearts of the prophets He chose. When reading Jonah, I clearly understood that God is truly almighty, that He hears the inner thoughts of non-believers and even uses what may appear on the surface as random situations to bring about His will.

For me, the Bible is 100 per cent truth without a single error. There are many parts of it that are difficult to comprehend, but that is strictly because of the human inability to understand, not because the Bible is erroneous in any way.

When saying that the Bible doesn't contain a single error, I refer to the contextual message of the Bible. It doesn't mean that other versions of the Scriptures or different expressions used in various translations of the Bible should be dismissed. I have compared a number of Korean translations with the English Bible and found small differences in each book, but when looking at the whole context, I did not see these as problematic.

For instance, in the four gospels (Matthew, Mark, Luke, and John), Jesus likens a rich man's entering heaven to a camel's going through an eye of a needle. In the Greek version of the Bible, the word *camel* can be mistaken for the word *rope* because of the difference of a single diacritical mark. But then isn't it true that both ropes and camels cannot pass through the eye of a needle? Whichever Bible version you may read, you see that it contains the same message as others when you look at it contextually.

Within the context of the truth that it is the Word of God, and with the key issue and message clear, different Bible versions may show slight differences in expression. Focusing only on the text and claiming it to be false is like staring at a tree and missing the scenery of the forest.

Second, the Bible was written through the inspiration of God. That is why many different writers from different periods of history wrote about the same message with complete consistency. As the Bible was inspired by God, the numerous writers, regardless of their historical period or location, were able to testify about Jesus Christ in uniform fashion.

The Bible is a book that was recorded by many people, each in different places, during a time period ranging from 1500 BC to 90 AD. Even so, the justice of God, His love, and the completion of the work of salvation are prophesied and testified to consistently in the Bible. Also, making references to biblical verses during His public life, Jesus accepted the authority of the Bible. He taught His disciples by using the Old Testament, such as by mentioning the burning thorn bush of Moses, the words of Isaiah, and the words of the psalmists.

In this way, the Bible transforms us with righteousness and makes them proper through God's teaching. "All Scripture is God-breathed and is useful for teaching, rebuking, correcting and training in righteousness" (2 Timothy 3:16).

Third, the Bible is the living Word of God. God created the world through His Word, and the Bible says that this Word is God. "In the beginning was the Word, and the Word was with God, and the Word was God. He was with God in the beginning. Through him all things were made; without him nothing was made that has been made. In him was life, and that life was the light of all mankind" (John 1:1–4).

This is how knowing the Bible leads us to knowing God. The Bible gives people wisdom to live out their lives and educate them so that they become God's holy people. Therefore, if one spends every day reading the Bible and keeping close to its words, then it is the same as living in intimacy with God.

Fourth, the Bible is a book that transforms people. That said, reading it is difficult because it is hard to understand and boring at times. It is hard to grasp the significance of all the names and numbers lined up on page after page. Even if you open the Bible, determined to read through it, you end up closing it again when you're worn out or just sleepy. If you think of the Bible as a story of a land far away, it is impossible to understand it properly. That is why it is very important to accept the Words of God, who is at work in the daily lives of each and every one of us.

The Bible is relevant and applicable to our lives right now. Those who believe that God will personally become involved in their lives and wake them with the Holy Spirit will ultimately experience great transformation.

People whose lives have been transformed after reading the Bible are scattered all over the world and are so many in number that they cannot be counted. The very book that changes people and provides the answers to the questions of life is the Bible.

Fifth, the Bible is a hidden secret. That is why both the wise and foolish cannot read the words- because the words are sealed. "So is my word that goes out from my mouth: It will not return to me empty, but will accomplish what I desire and achieve the purpose for which I sent it" (Isaiah 55:11).

As it says in Isaiah, the Bible isn't a book that anyone can easily understand and digest. Many people try to put the Bible into their own frameworks based on what they call experimental and verifiable facts of academic studies, such as biology, anthropology, history, and archaeology. When they find parts that do not fit, they claim that the Bible is erroneous.

The question of whether the Bible is true or erroneous has been a subject of debate even after the selection of the sixty-six legitimate books. To add to the flame, there are some among even eminent theologians who claim that the Bible is partly erroneous and do not believe it completely.

When it comes down to it, it can be concluded that such people who claim that the Bible is inaccurate do not have faith and do not believe in God. When we use the true-or-false mechanism in mathematics, we see that something containing 0.0001 per cent of an untruth is decisively false. In the same way, if something is not 100 per cent real, then it can only be false.

When people take only a portion of the Bible and interpret it literally, they end up hitting a wall. This was the very mistake I made in the past. Taking a portion out of context and instigating an argument based on that reminds me of Buddha's parable of a group of unseeing "blind" men fighting about an elephant.

As the story goes, blind people do not fully understand the full volume that is the elephant. Their knowledge of the elephant can only be partial, given their blindness. What kind of information each blind person has received about the elephant affects his or her perception of the huge creature. However, if each blind person with his partial knowledge were to insist that he or she was right and the others were wrong, it would be ridiculously foolish. If they all were to see the actual elephant in its full form, they would need sight. In this way, rather than taking parts of the Bible and arguing with only partial facts, we must seek the guidance of God's Spirit and trust only in Him with humble minds.

> These are the things God has revealed to us by his Spirit. The Spirit searches all things, even the deep things of God. For who knows a person's thoughts except their own spirit within them? In the same way no one knows the thoughts of God except the Spirit of God. What we have received is not the spirit of the world, but the Spirit who is from God, so that we may understand what God has freely given us. This is what we speak, not in words taught us by human wisdom but in words taught by the Spirit, explaining spiritual realities with Spirit-taught words. The person without the Spirit does not accept the things that come from the Spirit of God but considers them foolishness, and cannot understand them because they are discerned only through the Spirit. (1 Corinthians 2:10–14)

> "Above all, you must understand that no prophecy of Scripture came about by the prophet's own interpretation of things. For prophecy never had its origin in the human will, but prophets, though human, spoke from God as they were carried along by the Holy Spirit" (2 Peter 1:20–21).

Thus, the Bible is without a fault and must be taken in faith as the Words of God. Once a person reads the Bible with a humble mind and in reverence, his or her eyes and ears are opened, and then he or she gains an understanding of the Bible.

Sixth, the Bible surpasses all dimensions. The Bible has a way of moving people's hearts in individualised ways. This is why every person on earth can be moved by God's Words in a way that specifically touches the heart, regardless of whether the person is ignorant or educated, poor or rich.

God is a deity of a dimension that we cannot possibly fathom. The Bible explains how God has worked throughout the history of humankind, through human language, in a way that is simple.

For instance, the most high-dimensional and difficult theories of physics are often the most simple in nature. However, within their simplicity, there are many complex equations and laws of physics that are included. In the same way, the Bible has an impact with its text alone, but it is also multifaceted. Once you start understanding the contextual significance, the wondrous authority of God is made evident. Although you may not understand the Bible in the beginning, if you read it with consistent effort, you will be able to understand the high-dimensional truths through the light of the Holy Spirit.

Seventh, there is nothing missing from the Bible, and everything it says is backed up. "Look in the scroll of the Lord and read: None of these will be missing, not one will lack her mate. For it is his mouth that has given the order, and his Spirit will gather them together" (Isaiah 34:16).

Eighth, the Bible is not only a religious text but also a record of historical facts. It is a book that contains the message of a God who chose the Israelite nation as a sample in His plan to save humankind. Also, it reveals a God who individually meets each and every person, from Adam, Enoch, Noah, Abraham, Isaac, and Jacob to Joseph.

Richard Dawkins may dismiss the Bible as a made-up novel past its sell-by date, but the Bible is, in fact, the precise, accurate Word of God. The characters in it were real people who lived in history. It also doesn't magnify or glamorise such figures as great people but candidly describes them as they were, linking up the stories of their lives to the history of the world.

The ancestors of faith such as Abraham, Isaac, Jacob, David, and Solomon all had their weaknesses. However, God, who reached out to them first in His love and even called them righteous and "His friends" based upon their faith, does not turn His back on humans when they seek Him and call out to Him.

In reality, the Bible is a tear-jerking account of God's unreciprocated love towards humans. The cross of Jesus is the peak of the story, to which the entire Bible points.

It was Jesus that Moses and the Old Testament prophets pointed to, and it was He that the twelve disciples and apostles testified about.

Both the Old and New Testaments sum up to a single word: Jesus. Faith eventually brings eternal life, and this is gained through Jesus Christ. Jesus Himself said that He is the Bread of Life and the Way to eternal life.

> "You study the Scriptures diligently because you think that in them you have eternal life. These are the very Scriptures that testify about me" (John 5:39).

> "Now this is eternal life: that they know you, the only true God, and Jesus Christ, whom you have sent" (John 17:3).

> "Jesus answered, 'I am the way and the truth and the life. No one comes to the Father except through me'" (John 14:6).

There is no other path to salvation except the way of Jesus. When God spoke to Moses through the burning bush, He introduced Himself as "I am who I am." This reveals the characteristics of the Holy Trinity, which a Christian must possess, becoming a model of faith through the example of Abraham, a figure who signifies faith; Isaac, who was an image of Jesus Christ, the pure, blameless Lamb; and Jacob, a man who had both characteristics of faith and obedience. There is no other way to receive salvation, not through any foreign religion or beliefs of those whose bloodlines are not accepted by God.

This is why the Bible emphasises the genealogy of faith. God made this very clear. He proclaimed Himself as the God of Abraham and Isaac, not the God of Abraham, Ishmael and Muhammad. In this, the genealogy of faith shows that believing in Jesus is the only way to salvation.

The Bible is a book that explains all these truths by providing historical facts and analogies. Without this book, it is not possible to gain proper knowledge of God.

The Words of Jesus are the very source of living water, which never runs out, and the supplement of life that will relieve us of our spiritual thirst. It was not physical food that the Israelites ate before eventually dying in the desert, but it was the hidden manna of the soul that is essential for spiritual living.

CHAPTER 28

The Human Error

Regarding God, Richard Dawkins famously claimed, "The God of the Old Testament is arguably the most unpleasant character in all fiction: jealous and proud of it; a petty, unjust, unforgiving control-freak; a vindictive, bloodthirsty ethnic cleanser; a misogynistic, homophobic, racist, infanticidal, genocidal, filicidal, pestilential, megalomaniacal, sadomasochistic, capriciously malevolent bully."[1]

Dawkins' remark refers to the period when the Israelites were invading the land of Canaan and God told Joshua, the leader, to kill the Amorites regardless of whether they were male, female, slaves, or cattle. However, Dawkins is very much mistaken in his claim.

The God revealed in the Old Testament is a God of justice. He taught humans the law, showing just how daunting the matter of sin is. On the surface, we see that God's command to Joshua to kill the Canaanites is a historical fact. However, this incident contains the significance of eradicating the very root of sin in the mind when entering the kingdom of heaven, the spiritual land of Canaan. If people didn't remove all traces of sin, then these traces would once again cause the mind to rot. Joshua, in the Old Testament, was a figure symbolising Jesus, and the advancement into Canaan signifies the march of spiritual citizens entering the world of eternity.

As God showed the prophet Ezekiel, He is an almighty God who can revive to life even a pile of dried-up bones in a cave.

A lifetime is like a single day, with every aspect of it meaningless when compared to the spiritual world. The thoughts of humankind and those of God are in completely different dimensions.

The lesson God teaches humankind through the loss of these many lives is about the salvation of the soul and bear descendants of holiness, but those who do not realise this will not only die physically but will also not escape the terrible punishment that will fall upon them by the judgement of all eternity.

The march into Canaan and the ostentatious defeat of the Canaanites is an outward incident that on the surface teaches us how we should completely remove the seed of sin by pulling it out by the root when we are on the spiritual battleground.

God teaches us that we must relentlessly root out the seed of sin. Otherwise, in time, it will grow and bring about the destruction of the soul.

Because God's justice was shown through His unsparing punishment in the conquest of Canaan, Dawkins labels God as a god of war. Dawkins fails to realise the true sorrow in God's heart.

God's warnings about sin and punishment were not intended to kill but to save. When parents teach their children, they do not caution their kids with warnings in order to punish them. In the same way that parents cannot stand to see their children in danger, God commands people to keep His laws for purposes of their own happiness and salvation. In this, He is telling us to select life and His blessings, rejecting death and wrath.

> This day I call the heavens and the earth as witnesses against you that I have set before you life and death, blessings and curses. Now choose life, so that you and your children may live and that you may love the Lord your God, listen to his voice, and hold fast to him. For the Lord is your life, and he will give you many years in the land he swore to give to your fathers, Abraham, Isaac and Jacob. (Deuteronomy 30:19–20)

The reason God gave this command was to grant His people life.

A truly bloodthirsty god of sin who is haughty and engages in ethnic cleansing would not take this kind of measure. What God truly loves is the hatred of sin. Today, our minds contain all sorts of sinful characteristics like the tribes of Canaanites who lingered in the land. In order to enter the kingdom of heaven, we must fight against the evil in ourselves. If we do not remove all sin to the very root, then we fail in the spiritual conquest of Canaan.

The God of the Old Testament is unbending in His justice, and the God of the New Testament shows unconditional love. If justice could be set aside, then Jesus would not have had to come to the world and suffer the pain of the cross. However, while God is complete in His justice, He is also complete in love.

If justice was fully realised, then there wouldn't be a single sinful human soul or body remaining alive (Psalm 14:1–3; 53:1–3). However, God is the form of love and could fulfil both conditions through the death of Jesus Christ, who was completely human but without sin. Only that which is without fault and complete can be given as a sacrifice for sin. As a symbol of the coming Messiah, the priests gave offerings of animals for the atonement of sin.

However, in the times of the New Testament, Jesus came to the world and completely fulfilled the law by offering Himself up as a sacrifice for atonement, taking on the role of a high priest. This is why there is no longer a need for formalities like the sin offerings of the Old Testament.

> "Christ is the culmination of the law so that there may be righteousness for everyone who believes" (Romans 10:4).

> "By setting aside in his flesh the law with its commands and regulations. His purpose was to create in himself one new humanity out of the two, thus making peace" (Ephesians 2:15).

God is not unjust but is complete in His justice. At the same time, He is the God of complete love. No matter how evil a sinner a person may be, if he or she were simply to repent, then God would redirect that person from the road to judgement onto the path of His will. Examples of this truth can be found in various places in the Bible, including the judgement of Nineveh, as well as in the stories of many other figures in the Bible who repented and were cleared from judgement. "Now reform your ways and your actions and obey the Lord your God. Then the Lord will relent and not bring the disaster he has pronounced against you" (Jeremiah 26:13).

People must not make wrong assumptions about God through human misunderstanding. People selected by God walk to Him in faith, while those who are spiritually dead in their disbelief of His Word reject Him of their own accord. That is why claims that God is racist and discriminatory are wholly unfounded.

God is an almighty God who is far greater than what humans could possibly imagine. No matter how grand or vast a person's thoughts may be, compared to God, they do not even amount to a single grain of sand. "'For my thoughts are not your thoughts, neither are your ways my ways,' declares the Lord. 'As the heavens are higher than the earth, so are my ways higher than your ways and my thoughts than your thoughts'" (Isaiah 55:8–9).

God rejects an arrogant heart. People with such prideful minds inevitably face judgement. "For God did not send his Son into the world to condemn the world, but to save the world through him. Whoever believes in him is not condemned, but whoever does not believe stands condemned already because they have not believed in the name of God's one and only Son" (John 3:17–18).

However, as a person gets to know the Bible, he or she will move towards God with a humble heart. Plato said that it was impossible to theoretically prove transcendental ideas like the concepts of God, freedom, and a world of eternity. However, the Bible proves such cases in a manner that is easily comprehensible.

It made me very happy to think that the findings of historic philosophers and great thinkers resulting from years and years of deep contemplation and research could be accessed so easily and readily. That is why I read books of philosophy whenever I found the time. It is also how I came across several books of Bertrand Russell. While reading his works, I realised the fact that even the mind and rationality of a genius can be narrow. Between the lines of Russell's intellectual and logical sentences were narrow-minded reasoning and self-righteousness.

Also in his writings, he claimed that the concept of God had been formed out of absolutist societies of the Middle East, but this is untrue. He also said that the world must be conquered through human intelligence, but this is impossible. If it were feasible for the world to be taken over by pure intelligence, then why do we live in a world where footballers are more glorified than great philosophers?

The world cannot be conquered by human intellect. Also, even when intelligence is at its peak, it cannot change the way the world works. No matter how clever a person is, he or she does not stand in much comparison to a barbarian and does not even show up as a mere spot in the light of God's infinity and brilliance.

With the development of civilisations and science, the arrogance of humankind has mounted to the heavens as they have taken on cynical and mocking attitudes towards God. Many people think that science and God are unrelated. They also feel burdened about the subject of God in itself. That is why they look at you as if you are some alien from space when you start talking about Jesus and the cross. It is as though they think religion is ridiculous in the current generation of high technology that is continuing to race towards the future.

These people view science and religion as complete opposites, but the truth is that God and science are not separate. God Himself is extremely scientific and surpasses the highest point of any discoveries and technological developments. He is at the highest dimension and the pinnacle of philosophy and science—from where He looks down at humans and waits for them to break out of their arrogance and ignorance. "Though the Lord is exalted, he looks kindly on the lowly; though lofty, he sees them from afar" (Psalm 138:6).

In order for the reason of humankind to expand and gain more knowledge, people must realise the existence of God. For instance, when learning about probabilities in mathematics and accounting, you come to understand the reason and logic of physics, such as the uncertainty principle, parallel universes, and a multiverse, and ultimately start to realise the greatness of God and the small and utter weakness of humans.

However, some people use their accumulated knowledge in order to oppose God in their arrogance. The avarice of humankind has built up another Baal (a foreign god), which they claim as science, depending upon it and even revering it as if technology were a god.

These types of people even destroy nature and, as a result, suffer from the ramifications, such as natural disasters and pollution, which come back to them like a boomerang.

In conclusion, academic subjects like philosophy and science are extremely useful in terms of developing human intelligence and can be utilised as tools for deepening one's spirituality in finding God. However, this doesn't mean that such subjects should become idolised.

It is good to make use of technology when needed. However, there is a limit to human intelligence. Up to this point in time, academic, anthropologic, societal, economic, and scientific knowledge has not been made fully concrete. Humans are still in the stages of discovery in all aspects, and that is why we must keep on learning with a humble attitude.

Michio Kaku, a scholar of theoretical physics, described his profound spiritual experiences by saying, "Instead of being overwhelmed by the universe, I think that perhaps one of the deepest experiences a scientist can have, almost approaching a religious awakening, is to realize that we are children of the stars, and that our minds are capable of understanding the universal laws that they obey."[2]

Science and philosophy are not in opposition to God. In fact, it is in such studies that the presence of God is made all the more visible.

In various parts of the Bible, there are concepts of theoretical physics hidden here and there. These include Einstein's general theory of relativity and special theory of relativity as well as the Heisenberg and Schrödinger principles, not to mention the superstring theory that ties all of these together.

During Daniel's time, for instance, the hand that King Belshazzar saw writing on the wall was a phenomenon very similar to Michio Kaku's description of higher dimensions in his book *Hyperspace*. Other miraculous biblical events, such as Elijah's ascension to heaven, Jesus' body going through the sealed doors, Paul's prison door being unlocked, and others show consistency with the high-dimensional theories of physics.

Simply said, God embodies both the natural and the supernatural.

The episode of creation in Genesis makes it clear that the concept of a day for God is completely different in dimension from the twenty-four-hour day of a human being. The earth we are living on is a tiny planet, a microscopic speck of dust among the myriad stars on the outskirts of countless vast galaxies. On planet earth, we each live as an existence that is smaller than a single dot. In the light of this "universal" perspective, there could not be a more unbelievably miraculous evolution than this ability to even think about the existence of a God.

CHAPTER 29

Understanding beyond Our Dimension

> So we have to be aware of the possibility that there may be some things with explanations that we could never grasp, and maybe others with no explanation at all.[1]
>
> —Paul Davies, *The Mind of God*

Michio Kaku, a scholar of theoretical physics and a professor at New York University, claims that it is impossible to explain about a totally different dimension with the following analogy. He depicted a situation where a fish in a lily pond decided to jump out of the water. When it went back underwater and tried to explain about the world outside to its friends, it could find no way to express the world above the waters. Also, as fish do not have the same respiratory functions as humans do, Mr. Fish could not have had any way of explaining the existence of humans either. Even if he attempted to explain as eloquently as possible, other fish underwater would not understand beyond what he could explain.

Take a two-dimensional picture of a bird, for instance. Within a 2-D frame, or on a piece of paper, a three-dimensional bird could not be expressed in its living form. We cannot contain a bird's three-dimensional respiratory system on a single sheet of paper. That is why it is impossible to explain a living, breathing creature in the context of a two-dimensional world.

Another example we might think of is an elephant with an ant on its back. The ant only understands the two-dimensional world of moving across a flat surface in a straight line. The ant can't determine whether it is crawling across a wall or an elephant. Even if it were to realise that the wall and the elephant are different surfaces, it would never be able to fully know of the elephant's physique from head to toe. This is because the optical range of the ant is limited and it is simply impossible to see the complete elephant, which is incomparably larger than the ant's own tiny form.

But let's say that this ant could somehow look far ahead and had the ability to fly. High up in the sky, it would be able to set its eyes upon vast scenery that cannot be explained adequately in the world of ants. Landing back on the ground, the ant may try to describe the elephant to its friend, but the friend that has spent its entire life on the surface of a flat world would not be able to even fathom, let alone believe in, the shape or size of the three-dimensional creature called the elephant. In this sense, it is almost impossible to describe a dimension that is different from one's own.

However, the Bible explains the material world and other, spiritual dimensions in a way that humans can easily understand. It is a book that leaps beyond dimensional constraints.

Even in our contemporary world, there is a variety of timely, spatial, cultural, and mental dimensions. We could say that a person living a primitive life in the Amazon lives in a completely different dimension from the urban person with the smartest, fastest technology of the day.

For instance, what would happen if we were to enter the Amazon and start talking to a tribesman who had never come across a civilised person in a language he could not understand? We would be treated as some sort of fanatic alien and be chased out or even killed. Even if we were to communicate with the tribespeople after learning to speak their tongue, we would have no way of knowing how much they would believe about our world in which the peak development of science and technology allows us to fly around space. We cannot imagine how they would respond if we were to explain about electronic technology to those who still use rocks and sticks as tools.

However, God has effortlessly explained the material dimension and other, spiritual worlds to humans in their very own language. The Bible reveals truths about the world of different dimensions that can only stand to amaze.

Paul said that he witnessed a sight that couldn't be explained in words when he saw a man taken to the "third heaven," as described in 2 Corinthians. At the time, he didn't know whether the man was in his body or was having an out-of-body experience. However, Paul did mention a supernatural world. As his testimony declares, this spiritual world of another dimension that is "unable to be described in words" is surely in existence. Also, there is judgement based on our faith and actions.

God places in us a heart that yearns for eternity and allows us to discover the mysterious world of souls. Although it is a difficult task to understand a completely different dimension of being, God has spoken to us in a way that is comprehensible to us. The Bible describes an amazing spiritual world and fills us with the strength for and hope of an eternal afterlife through our current struggles and suffering. We can also become people who are able to forgive the most insufferable person and give to others rather than receive.

People who love God come to love their brothers. Sins such as telling lies, being jealous, being greedy, committing adultery, theft, or murder, and bearing false witness, come to light. People who love their fellows bear fruit of the Holy Spirit and live overflowing with love, peace, joy, mercy, goodness, faithfulness, gentleness, self-control, and thanksgiving. Those who live this kind of life are people who have transcended this world and reached one of a higher dimension. This dimension that non-believers cannot ever know of is a world of the heavens filled with joy and peace. It is a world that is already in our hearts. We who have the fruit of the Spirit walk the path of life, taking each step on the earth, but within our minds, we are already the people of heaven.

CHAPTER 30

God Seeks Us First

It is impossible for people to fully know God's existence or to successfully seek Him out entirely on their own. That is why God approaches humans first.

Even when we were sinners under the impending judgement that is to come, God loved us and wanted to save us. Becoming a sin offering in place of humans was a measure He had to take in order to save us. This came in the form of the cross, which manifested God's perfect love and, at the same time, fulfilled His complete righteousness.

While I was a sinner, God came to find me first. And He asked me the ontological question that He had once asked Adam in the beginning. People tend to ask why God had to come to the world only to suffer tremendous pain upon the cross. They also ask that if He really is almighty, then why didn't He save the world with His supernatural powers instead of complicating things with the cross and resurrection?

Moreover, one comes to wonder how humans are supposed to realise that an invisible God has given them salvation.

Let's say that an isolated tribe in the Amazon is going to be hit by an atomic bomb within the next few days. The Amazonians are completely unaware of their impending doom, but a president of a nearby country knows about it and has a plan to save them. The president flies over by helicopter and tells the people, in his native tongue, that he is going to save them. Would the Amazonians thank him and get on the helicopter straightaway? Unable to understand what he is saying, they would simply refuse to follow him. If he tried to force them onto the helicopter to save them, they would probably seize him and burn him up.

Similarly, in order to save humankind, God had to take certain steps in order to get through to humans. First, He had to communicate through the language that they used and explain to them in ways that they could understand. So God chose a certain period of time and a space within history and came to the world in the body of a man. Instead of taking on a supernatural form, He came as an ordinary man named Jesus, son of a carpenter. Through the body of young Mary, He came in a state completely free of Adam's Original Sin, which is embedded in all people, and became a sin offering for humankind, spilling His precious, flawless blood.

The fact that the God of everything had to come down to the level of humankind and endure all its constraints and limitations must have been suffering enough, much more painful than the cross. As if this were not enough, Jesus Christ was born in the lowest, most humble way imaginable and experienced the highest form of human agony and pain before He tragically died on the cross at age thirty-three. "For God so loved the world that he gave his one and only Son, that whoever believes in him shall not perish but have eternal life" (John 3:16).

Anyone who calls upon the name of Jesus gains salvation. Jesus is the Way of life, the Word of Truth, and the true physical form of God through whom we can gain eternal life. No other religious figure in the world made such a bold declaration about himself. Jesus is the only source of salvation for us here on earth. In Acts, it clearly states that there is no other name that is given to us. That is why we can only be doomed to travel the cursed road of failure if we stray away from Jesus. "Kiss his son, or he will be angry and your way will lead to your destruction, for his wrath can flare up in a moment. Blessed are all who take refuge in him" (Psalm 2:12).

To "kiss his son" signifies a person who accepts Jesus Christ as his or her Saviour and acknowledges Him with his or her lips.

God made Himself known to humanity through His Word. He approached humans first, after preparing the road of salvation through Jesus Christ. God does not reveal Himself to humans by some mysterious, supernatural means, but He meets each and every one of us, personally and individually in our lives. God seeks out a person first and stands knocking at the door of his or her heart.

The words of the Bible proclaim faith based on "today" and "now." If we are to hear God's voice here and now, on this very day, then we must respond to His calling at once and repent of our past actions, returning to Him with a brand new heart. "'Even now,' declares the Lord, 'return to me with all your heart, with fasting and weeping and mourning.' Rend your heart and not your garments. Return to the Lord your God, for he is gracious and compassionate, slow to anger and abounding in love, and he relents from sending calamity" (Joel 2:12–13).

CHAPTER 31

Why God Gave Us the Law

Before the fall of humankind, God gave the command not to eat from the Tree of Good and Evil. After the fall, He clothed Adam and Eve with the skin of a slaughtered animal. This was a sign that God had given humankind a set of laws.

Moses received God's instructions inscribed on the stone tablets and passed them on to the Israelite people. For non-Israelites, however, God also showed His justice through certain standards based on their conscience. There were reasons why God had exclusively chosen the Israelite people as a sample and handed them the law through Moses. First, it was in order to make people understand the concept of sin. "Therefore no one will be declared righteous in God's sight by the works of the law; rather, through the law we become conscious of our sin" (Romans 3:20).

While the law, on its own, can make people realise why certain actions have been categorised as sin, it ultimately does not eradicate the sin itself. God placed all humankind under the law in order to make humans understand His completeness and justice. Without law, it is impossible to determine what is or isn't sin.

> "To be sure, sin was in the world before the law was given, but sin is not charged against anyone's account where there is no law" (Romans 5:13).

> "Now we know that whatever the law says, it says to those who are under the law, so that every mouth may be silenced and the whole world held accountable to God" (Romans 3:19).

On the other hand, for the nations that did not know the law, God provided a way for them to discover His goodness through their own conscience. "'Am I only a God nearby,' declares the Lord, 'and not a God far away'" (Jeremiah 23:23)?

> The God who made the world and everything in it is the Lord of heaven and earth and does not live in temples built by human hands. And he is not served by human hands, as if he needed anything. Rather, he himself gives everyone life and breath and everything else. From one man he made all the nations, that they should inhabit the whole earth; and he marked out their appointed times in history and the boundaries of their lands. God did this so that they would seek him and perhaps reach out for him and find him, though he is not far from any one of us. (Acts 17:24–27)

God's presence fills the entire universe. He knows every being on earth, whether they be Christian or atheist. He desires for them to realise their sins and turn around their lives for good.

Second, the law was given for humans to cultivate the "field" of their minds.

Among the many parables in the Bible, there is one where God likens Himself to an owner of a vineyard. Jesus, telling this story, repeats several times, "My Father is a farmer," saying this in a metaphoric sense.

As He told us to rule over ourselves, He expressed this figuratively, saying that we should "cultivate our fields," comparing the state of our minds to either a wasteland or a good landscape.

As we live our lives in deserted wastelands and on rugged rocks since the fall of Adam and Eve, we humans must take care of our fields to make fertile ground like the garden of Eden, which was full of joy and splendour.

That is how we will be able to grow sprouts of God's Word and bear abundant fruit.

> "This is what the Lord says to the people of Judah and to Jerusalem: 'Break up your unplowed ground and do not sow among thorns. Circumcise yourselves to the Lord, circumcise your hearts, you people of Judah and inhabitants of Jerusalem, or my wrath will flare up and burn like fire because of the evil you have done—burn with no one to quench it'" (Jeremiah 4:3–4).

> "Sow righteousness for yourselves, reap the fruit of unfailing love, and break up your unplowed ground; for it is time to seek the Lord, until he comes and showers his righteousness on you" (Hosea 10:12).

Third, the law was the shadow of the Jesus, the coming Messiah.

Moses and the prophets of the Old Testament all prophesied about the coming of Jesus, the Saviour and Messiah. The law merely casts the shadow, lacking the fullness of Jesus Himself, who is ultimately God and the Word. However, after Jesus came and dwelt among us, the Israelites still clung to the shadow, thereby committing the serious error of failing to recognise Jesus as the true and complete form of God.

> "The law is only a shadow of the good things that are coming—not the realities themselves. For this reason it can never, by the same sacrifices repeated endlessly

> year after year, make perfect those who draw near to worship" (Hebrews 10:1).
>
> "Now faith is confidence in what we hope for and assurance about what we do not see. This is what the ancients were commended for" (Hebrews 11:1–2).
>
> "Why, then, was the law given at all? It was added because of transgressions until the Seed to whom the promise referred had come. The law was given through angels and entrusted to a mediator" (Galatians 3:19).

God bestowed the law upon humans so that, through the standards categorising sin, humans would understand and be able to differentiate what is and is not sin. Thus, the human mind, like a wasteland covered with thorn bushes, would become a field of fertile soil in which the Word could grow out from the planted seed and ultimately receive Jesus Christ, who will shine upon us the Words of light.

God also wants us to bear abundant fruit that is full of light and make up a holy congregation to be saved. However, the Israelites stubbornly held onto the outdated words of Moses and abided by the law in appearance only. In their hearts, they were full to the brim with jealousy, avarice, and sin so much so that they crucified the Messiah who had come in the form of love.

In spite of this, in all His wisdom and patience, God used this situation to open up the doors of salvation to the world so that whoever simply puts faith in Jesus is given the grace of becoming His disciple.

CHAPTER 32

The Blood of the Cross and the Sin of Humankind

> For the life of a creature is in the blood, and I have given it to you to make atonement for yourselves on the altar; it is the blood that makes atonement for one's life.
>
> —Leviticus 17:11

Throughout the Old Testament, the blood of an animal was needed for the forgiveness of sin. The price of sin was death; thus, those who sinned would have to die. However, this meant that there would not be even a single person left alive in the world, as no one is without sin. So God required the blood of an animal to take the place of humankind's blood as payment for sin. As there is life in blood and as blood covers up sin, people were to take an animal's life to pay for their own transgressions.

In this situation, people should have genuinely repented with their hearts as they watched an animal bleed to death for their deadly sins, in their place. However, this offering became a systematic practice through which people slaughtered animals without feeling genuine sorrow and contriteness for what they had done. God could no longer stand to watch them carry on as they were, so He sent prophets in order to warn them about their pretence.

> "The multitude of your sacrifices—what are they to me?" says the Lord. "I have more than enough of burnt offerings, of rams and the fat of fattened animals; I have no pleasure in the blood of bulls and lambs and goats. When you come to appear before me, who has asked this of you, this trampling of my courts? Stop bringing meaningless offerings! Your incense is detestable to me. New Moons, Sabbaths and convocations—I cannot bear your worthless assemblies. (Isaiah 1:11–13)

> "'Oh, that one of you would shut the temple doors, so that you would not light useless fires on my altar! I am not pleased with you,' says the Lord Almighty, 'and I will accept no offering from your hands'" (Malachi 1:10).

In all honesty, what would God, the Creator of all things, expect from the hands of mere humans? Rather than coming to true repentance, by watching living creatures die for their sins in sacrifice, the evil nature of humankind worsened to the point where God proclaimed that He would rather have the temple closed down.

Malachi was the last prophet of the Old Testament. He prophesied that Elijah would come before the Messiah. Approximately four hundred years later, during the generation of King Herod and Caiaphas the high priest, and six months prior to Jesus' birth, John the Baptist was born.

Jesus, who is the eternal High Priest in the Order of Melchizedek, did away with the ritualistic sacrifices, bringing humankind the ultimate forgiveness of sin. That is why after Jesus' single act upon the cross, anyone can approach the throne of God through faith. "Where our forerunner, Jesus, has entered on our behalf. He has become a high priest forever, in the order of Melchizedek" (Hebrews 6:20).

Beyond comparison to the blood of animals, which had to be shed time and time again, Jesus' blood was an invaluable, priceless offering. Even a single drop of His blood was enough to cover the sin of humankind, yet He bled profusely as he died on the cross. There is simply no other way for one to be saved except by the name of Jesus, who came into the history of humankind in order to complete the plan of redemption through the shedding of His blood on the cross. "Salvation is found in no one else, for there is no other name under heaven given to mankind by which we must be saved" (Acts 4:12).

Therefore, in order to be forgiven of sin, a person must believe in the gospel of Jesus and repent. For the generations of people who did not know about this gospel, God permitted them to go their own way. However, He has called all people of earth to repent and has given us the evidence by which we can have faith in Him. "In the past God overlooked such ignorance, but now he commands all people everywhere to repent. For he has set a day when he will judge the world with justice by the man he has appointed. He has given proof of this to everyone by raising him from the dead" (Acts 17:30–31).

However, the Israelites did not realise that John the Baptist, with the heart of Elijah, had come in preparation of the Messiah. Neither did they recognise Jesus as the Messiah. Although they knew the Bible inside out, reading the Scriptures day and night, they couldn't recognise Jesus and ended up having him hung Him on the cross, condemning Him by way of Roman law.

> "This man was handed over to you by God's deliberate plan and foreknowledge; and you, with the help of wicked men, put him to death by nailing him to the cross. But God raised him from the dead, freeing him from the agony of death, because it was impossible for death to keep its hold on him" (Acts 2:23–24).

> "You disowned the Holy and Righteous One and asked that a murderer be released to you. You killed the

author of life, but God raised him from the dead. We are witnesses of this" (Acts 3:14–15).

Today, the news of Jesus is being delivered to every corner of the earth. Despite this spread of the good news, there remain countless many who dismiss this message as a joke, like the sons-in-law of Lot, who was the nephew of Abraham. Such people either do not believe in Jesus or are repulsed by the wrongdoings of Christians.

This is a great tragedy, as those who do not take faith are the ones who have everything to lose in the end. If a person does not open his or her heart to Jesus, then only judgement awaits. When Jesus died on the cross, He went to spread the news to the souls confined in hell. Even to the people of Noah's time who died during the flood because of their disobedience, Jesus went to deliver the news. "After being made alive, he went and made proclamation to the imprisoned spirits—to those who were disobedient long ago when God waited patiently in the days of Noah while the ark was being built. In it only a few people, eight in all, were saved through water" (1 Peter 3:19–20).

As He hung upon the cross, Jesus spoke seven messages. In those messages, the mind of God, who saved the world, and His intentions were manifested. In the same way that a grain of wheat cannot produce life without decomposing first, Jesus' death gave humans life His Words remain alive to this day, bringing transformation to our lives.

And the Word of Jesus is a light that saves humankind. "In the beginning was the Word, and the Word was with God, and the Word was God. He was with God in the beginning. Through him all things were made; without him nothing was made that has been made. In him was life, and that life was the light of all mankind" (John 1:1–4).

This Word is alive and is the definition of life itself. Jesus' Word is light and life, containing the heart and mind of God. "The Spirit gives life; the flesh counts for nothing. The words I have spoken to you—they are full of the Spirit and life" (John 6:63). Consider this also: "What do you prefer? Shall I come to you with a rod of discipline, or shall I come in love and with a gentle spirit" (1 Corinthians 4:21)?

Therefore, Jesus' blood allows us to receive eternal life. Embodying the mind and thoughts of God, who is the Word and the Light of the World, the precious blood of Christ has the power to completely forgive the sins of humans in the past, present, and future.

CHAPTER 33

Melchizedek

As I read Hebrews 5, I saw the verse regarding Melchizedek, "Of whom we have much to say, and hard to explain, since you have become dull of hearing." My curiosity was piqued once again.

"We have much to say about this, but it is hard to make it clear to you because you no longer try to understand. In fact, though by this time you ought to be teachers, you need someone to teach you the elementary truths of God's word all over again. You need milk, not solid food" (Hebrews 5:11–12)!

As I perused the Scriptures to find the traces of Melchizedek, I found only three places in the entire Bible that spoke about the mysterious figure—in Genesis, Psalms, and Hebrews.

Melchizedek makes his first appearance in Genesis 14:18. When Lot was captured while living in Sodom, Abraham, with the company of several kings, fought and won a battle against Kedorlaomer to save his nephew Lot. After his victory, Melchizedek, the king of Salem, came to bless Abraham with bread and wine. "Then Melchizedek king of Salem brought out bread and wine. He was priest of God Most High, and he blessed Abram, saying, 'Blessed be Abram by God Most High, Creator of heaven and earth. And praise be to God Most High, who delivered your enemies into your hand.' Then Abram gave him a tenth of everything" (Genesis 14:18–20).

Melchizedek appears for the second time in Psalm 110:4, where it is written, "You are a priest forever, in the order of Melchizedek."

The final mention of Melchizedek is in Hebrews, where he is described in greater detail than in any other passage in the Bible. From Hebrews 5 to Hebrews 8, there is an extensive explanation about Melchizedek. Chapters 9 and 10 add further explanations, leading into chapter 11, which lists the ancestors of faith who followed the "order of Melchizedek." "This Melchizedek was king of Salem and priest of God Most High. He met Abraham returning from the defeat of the kings and blessed him, and Abraham gave him a tenth of everything" (Hebrews 7:1–4).

First, the name Melchizedek means "king of righteousness"; also, "king of Salem" means "king of peace." Without father or mother, without genealogy, without beginning of days or end of life, and resembling the Son of God, Melchizedek remains a priest forever. Just think how great he was: Even the patriarch Abraham gave him a tenth of his plunder and was blessed by him (Hebrews 7:7).

Melchizedek, as mentioned in the Bible, is a high priest who is described as an eternal figure with "no father or mother, without genealogy, without beginning of days or end of life." He existed before Abraham's descendent Levi was born. In this, it can be said the high priest of the tribe of Levi paid his tenth through Abraham to Melchizedek, who is ultimately able to receive the tithe. With such characteristics, this figure is ultimately God and signifies Jesus Christ, who is the eternal High Priest. The Israelites had to offer annual sacrifices through the high priest to be forgiven of their sins, but with this practice's being the shadow of what was to come, it was only necessary until Jesus came as the fully fledged sacrifice. "They serve at a sanctuary that is a copy and shadow of what is in heaven. This is why Moses was warned when he was about to build the tabernacle: 'See to it that you make everything according to the pattern shown you on the mountain'" (Hebrews 8:5).

The rituals wherein the high priest offered up sacrifices each year only reminded the people of sin. The rituals did not remove sin permanently. "But those sacrifices are an annual reminder of sins. It is impossible for the blood of bulls and goats to take away sins" (Hebrews 10:3–4).

With the blood of an animal considered adequate to take away sin, the author of Hebrews expresses how much more effective the blood of Jesus is in washing away sin.

> The blood of goats and bulls and the ashes of a heifer sprinkled on those who are ceremonially unclean sanctify them so that they are outwardly clean. How much more, then, will the blood of Christ, who through the eternal Spirit offered himself unblemished to God, cleanse our consciences from acts that lead to death, so that we may serve the living God! (Hebrews 9:13–14)

Jesus did not follow the traditional order of the high priest under the law of the Old Testament but instead chose a point in time in which He completed the work of redemption once and for all (Hebrews 7:27). He was the Eternal High Priest in the Order of Melchizedek. "For it is declared: 'You are a priest forever, in the order of Melchizedek'" (Hebrews 7:17).

Today, those who believe in God receive the authority of becoming His own sons and daughters. We become a part of the division of high priests who follow the Order of Melchizedek, as Jesus did. In this contemporary world, taking on the role of a high priest in the Order of Melchizedek means that we must become a source of living light that shines upon souls in darkness through the Word of God. "In the same way, let your light shine before others, that they may see your good deeds and glorify your Father in heaven" (Matthew 5:16).

CHAPTER 34

Jesus' Seven Sayings upon the Cross

> I have set my rainbow in the clouds, and it will be the sign of the covenant between me and the earth.
>
> —Genesis 9:13

Jesus came according to the prophecies of the Old Testament and fulfilled them completely by dying on the cross. Isaiah 53 contains everything about Christ, from His appearance and works in life to His death on the cross as a sacrifice for sin. Instead of protesting or crying out in pain, Jesus spoke seven times. Reading the Bible, I wondered why Jesus had kept on speaking up until His death. While He was in excruciating pain, Jesus spoke seven significant messages, one by one, until He finally drew His last breath. This was truly extraordinary.

After the great flood, God made a promise to Noah with a rainbow. The seven things Jesus said on the cross signify the words of the covenant promised by God, marked by the seven colours of the rainbow—and the sayings lay out the very heart of the Bible.

The first time Jesus spoke, He asked for the forgiveness of non-believers for their ignorance. Israelites did not believe the fact that Jesus was the Messiah. Representing humankind, Jesus prayed for forgiveness on behalf of these people. "Therefore I will give him a portion among the great, and he will divide the spoils with the strong, because he poured out his life unto death, and was numbered with the transgressors. For he bore the sin of many, and made intercession for the transgressors" (Isaiah 53:12).

If sinners turn from the path of disbelief, then God, through Jesus Christ's plea on behalf of ignorant humankind, forgives them of their past wrongdoings and accepts them.

Second, Jesus' words promised the kingdom of heaven for repentant sinners. The sinner on the right side of Jesus repented of his sins and accepted Jesus as the Messiah. Upon his acceptance, Jesus responded to him immediately and promised he would go to heaven. This criminal did not listen to the other criminal on Jesus' left who insulted and mocked Jesus but admitted that while he was being punished for his crimes, Jesus was completely blameless. While His own disciples had deserted Christ, this criminal on His left accepted Jesus, a wretched, mangled form dangling upon the cross, as the Messiah. Setting his eyes on Jesus, he professed his faith, saying, "Jesus, remember me when you come into your kingdom."

In this day, too, those who accept Jesus as their Saviour through the confession of faith can enter through the gates of heaven. "Jesus answered him, 'Truly I tell you, today you will be with me in paradise'" (Luke 23:42).

Paradise is promised to all who accept Jesus as the Messiah and come to repentance. If those who hear the good news receive His calling and repent accordingly then they will receive the promise of paradise.

The third words of Jesus were in regards to His mother. Jesus requested that John, His disciple who was standing with His mother, take care of her. When a person believes in Jesus, he or she must respect his or her parents. In light of God's command to love Him and our neighbours, the closest neighbours we have are our parents. Without respecting them, we cannot live truly Christian lives. "When Jesus saw his mother there, and the disciple whom he loved standing nearby, he said to her, 'Woman, here is your son,' and to the disciple, 'Here is your mother.' From that time on, this disciple took her into his home" (John 19:26–27).

During Jesus' time, Israelites did not take care of their parents, offering the excuse that they had to make offerings to God, called Korban.

Until noon, when Jesus spoke for the third time, the day had been mild, but after His fourth saying, the clouds began to darken. "It was now about noon, and darkness came over the whole land until three in the afternoon" (Luke 23:44).

The tear across the curtain in the sanctuary signifies the end of sacrificial rituals through the priests in the Old Testament and marks the beginning of an era where anyone who calls upon the name of Jesus can enter confidently into the sanctuary.

The fourth words He spoke were, "Eli, Eli, lama sabachthani?" "About three in the afternoon Jesus cried out in a loud voice, 'Eli, Eli, lama sabachthani?' (which means 'My God, my God, why have you forsaken me?')" (Matthew 27:46; Mark 15:34). Compare this to one of David's psalms: "My God, my God, why have you forsaken me? Why are you so far from saving me, so far from my cries of anguish" (Psalm 22:1)?

The words Jesus spoke are usually spoken by humans who have sinned, so one naturally becomes curious about why Jesus had to say such a thing. Isaiah 53:12 provides the answer to this: "Therefore I will give him a portion among the great, and he will divide the spoils with the strong, because he poured out his life unto death, and was numbered with the transgressors. For he bore the sin of many, and made intercession for the transgressors."

Jesus, totally devoid of sin, was completely human and, at the same time, completely God. In the three-dimensional world, humans live with a four-dimensional concept of time. Jesus, who came into the world in the exact form, time, and space prophesied throughout the Old Testament, was devoid of sin, so He could not go to hell. However, He discarded His pure soul as He took on the sins of humankind so He could reach out to the sinners trapped in hell.

The words "My God, my God, why have you forsaken me?" refer to the pain caused by sin and separation from God, which is more terrible than physical death on the cross. Jesus referred to this outcry of sinful humans and descended into hell in order to save those who had died before the flood of Noah's time. "After being made alive, he went and made proclamation to the imprisoned spirits—to those who were disobedient long ago when God waited patiently in the days of Noah while the ark was being built. In it only a few people, eight in all, were saved through water" (1 Peter 3:19–20).

Jesus, who sought and preached the gospel even to the souls in hell, is not stuck between the pages of Israeli history. Instead, He is the true Messiah prevalent in the past, present, and future of humankind. Also, He resurrected and ascended into heaven in accordance with the words of the Scriptures. He is alive yesterday, today, and forever. Therefore, the prayer of blood and sweat in Gethsemane was one of pain from the writhing of His soul.

Jesus' disciples were completely clueless about what was going on. This was the case even for Jesus' closest disciples, Peter, John, and Jacob, who had listened to His words and teachings in the front lines. This trio could not even carry out Jesus' request to stay awake and pray. The disciples, who had followed Jesus for three years, were unable to truly understand His words and came to deny Him as He hung on the cross. Upon His death, they all scattered, each going his own way.

Even so, after His resurrection, Jesus called together these inadequate disciples once again and trained them for forty days as He remained on earth in His revitalised form, before ascending up to heaven. After experiencing the resurrected Christ, the disciples were born again as true followers of Jesus.

Therefore, a Christian must no longer hand Jesus over to the cross for his or her own gain or live a life denying Him but be born again as a true disciple and become an example to others. Christians who cannot confidently reveal their faith to others and who commit worse deeds than non-believers have no right to criticise Judah of Iscariot or any other disciple.

In this world where people frequently deny the name of Jesus, being drawn to riches, honour, power, and other things out of their greedy desire, we must be able to boldly relinquish such temptations and grab onto Jesus' hand. Like the eleven apostles who came onto the true path of discipleship after meeting the resurrected Christ, we must be born again with a new, transformed life of faith.

"Later, knowing that everything had now been finished, and so that Scripture would be fulfilled, Jesus said, 'I am thirsty'" (John 19:28). How was it that Jesus became thirsty when He is the source of living water? Remember that Jesus had asked the Samaritan woman at Jacob's well to fetch Him some water. Casually striking up a conversation appropriate to the time and place, Jesus told the woman that He was the very source of living water that never runs out.

The woman recognised that Jesus was the Messiah and spread the word throughout her village. By the time the disciples arrived at the scene, Jesus told them that there was already food prepared. The disciples didn't understand Him and thought He meant that someone had literally fetched Jesus something to eat. However, the food Jesus was referring to was the food of eternity. The food had come to carry out and fulfil the will of the One who had sent it.

Then the thirst Jesus was referring to was the thirst of the soul that He had felt because of His own disciples who did not believe He was the Messiah, even after ministering with Him tirelessly for three years. Although the Twelve followed Jesus around for three years, experiencing His miracles and wondrous abilities, they ended up betraying Him and scattering. Jesus, however, sought them out to steady them again. He loved them until the very end.

An incident that is reminiscent of Jesus' thirst is the thirst that David felt in the Old Testament. David longed for a drink from the well outside the gates of Bethlehem. However, because it was located in the heart of the Philistines' camp, he would have to infiltrate the enemies in order to get a single sip. David's three mighty warriors risked their lives and fought through the lines of the Philistine army so that they could bring to David a bowl of water from the well (1 Chronicles 11:17–19).

Even to this day, God feels thirst for those who do not believe in Him. Considering the way David's three warriors laid down their lives and devoted themselves for a mere human being, there is no excuse for why people should not dedicate themselves to God with the same, if not all the more, fervour and passion. Thus, those who are separated from God are in severe thirst, from a dehydrated soul.

However, with the blood Jesus spilled on the cross, we have become at peace with God and our souls are once again renewed through His Words.

Those who have left God have the thirst of the soul. However, there is now a way for the soul to revive through Jesus' Words of eternity by becoming reconciled with God through His precious blood on the cross.

Jesus' sixth words, "It is finished," refer to the completion of the work of salvation. "When he had received the drink, Jesus said, "It is finished." With that, he bowed his head and gave up his spirit" (John 19:30).

Jesus came to the world in accordance with the prophesies of the Old Testament, and upon the cross He completed His mission as the Saviour of the world. From the very beginning, He already knew everything had been fulfilled (John 19:28). In Genesis, God had said that the "descendant of a woman" would crush the Serpent's head. This was referring to the completion of redemption and the victory of God's Word. With creation, God already completed everything.

It was the redemption of humankind, the victory of Revelation, and the creation of a new earth and a new heaven that was completed as a part of the plan for salvation. When Jesus sent out His disciples, two by two, He told them that He had seen Satan fall from heaven like lightning (Luke 10:18).

Therefore, as those who believe in Him, we have already won the fight against Satan. That is why we can surely win spiritual battles against Satan. God is the Alpha and Omega, the Beginning and the End. He is an able God who sees and penetrates the future; He completed the historical work of salvation for all people, once and for all.

When Jesus spoke for the seventh and final time, He gave His soul to God. "Jesus called out with a loud voice, 'Father, into your hands I commit my spirit.' When he had said this, he breathed his last" (Luke 23:46). "Into your hands I commit my spirit; deliver me, Lord, my faithful God" (Psalm 31:5).

With words from the Scripture, Jesus entrusted His soul to God. He exemplified how we should all give our souls to the Father. Then Jesus rose from the dead, three days after He carried out his mission and ascended to Heaven. Revealing Himself to the Twelve after His resurrection, Jesus fed them with the spiritual food, teaching them the Word of God, and sent them out into the world to preach the news to the ends of the earth and to raise up disciples. "Therefore go and make disciples of all nations, baptizing them in the name of the Father and of the Son and of the Holy Spirit, and teaching them to obey everything I have commanded you. And surely I am with you always, to the very end of the age" (Matthew 28:19–20).

This is why we must hold His mission in our hearts and live to fulfil it as His disciples.

> In your relationships with one another, have the same mind set as Christ Jesus: Who, being in very nature God, did not consider equality with God something to be used to his own advantage; rather, he made himself nothing by taking the very nature of a servant, being made in human likeness. And being found in appearance as a man, he humbled himself by becoming obedient to death—even death on a cross! Therefore God exalted him to the highest place and gave him the name that is above every name, that at the name of Jesus every knee should bow, in heaven and on earth and under the earth, and every tongue acknowledge that Jesus Christ is Lord, to the glory of God the Father. (Philippians 2:5–11)

> "In the same way, let your light shine before others, that they may see your good deeds and glorify your Father in heaven" (Matthew 5:16).

CHAPTER 35

Standing before the Almighty

Every Sunday, there are so many people who pose as Christians as they step across the courtyard of a church. These people say they believe in God, but they remain in elementary faith, with one foot in the world, living uncertainly in compromise with its ways.

Although it may not seem like it, non-believers are silently watching these kinds of people. So if Christians fail to live exemplary lives, they will only cause non-believers to fall farther away from God. That is the reason why God wants His people to live as a light to the world in a complete and holy way of life.

> "When Abram was ninety-nine years old, the Lord appeared to him and said, 'I am God Almighty; walk before me faithfully and be blameless'" (Genesis 17:1).

> "You must be blameless before the Lord your God" (Deuteronomy 18:13).

> "Therefore let us move beyond the elementary teachings about Christ and be taken forward to maturity, not laying again the foundation of repentance from acts that lead to

death, and of faith in God, instruction about cleansing rites, the laying on of hands, the resurrection of the dead, and eternal judgment" (Hebrews 6:1–2).

Also, God tells us to "be holy, for [He is] holy." We, saints of the church, must please God through a holy way of living. If we are not holy, then we cannot see God. "Make every effort to live in peace with everyone and to be holy; without holiness no one will see the Lord" (Hebrews 12:14).

To humans, completeness and holiness seem like standards that are as high up and seemingly impossible to reach as God Himself. However, God requires this standard of conduct from His people.

Thus, we must become an example of integrity and holiness to non-believers as we live in this world ridden with evil. Also, as the children of God, who is holy, holiness must become our way of life. In Jude, it describes the prophecy of Enoch, the seventh descendant of Adam who went up to heaven without facing death. "Enoch, the seventh from Adam, prophesied about them: 'See, the Lord is coming with thousands upon thousands of his holy ones to judge everyone, and to convict all of them of all the ungodly acts they have committed in their ungodliness, and of all the defiant words ungodly sinners have spoken against him'" (Jude 1:14–15).

We are citizens of the kingdom of heaven. We are the sons and daughters of God and have also become "kinglike" priests. This is why we must live distinguished lives suited to our status in God's kingdom. This is what we call a holy life. "But our citizenship is in heaven. And we eagerly await a Savior from there, the Lord Jesus Christ" (Philippians 3:20).

We must discard all characteristics of this world: living in debauchery, lust, drunkenness, and orgies, carousing and being detestable. Instead, we must live each and every day in expectance of Christ, who, in heaven, sits in the throne of glory.

> "Since, then, you have been raised with Christ, set your hearts on things above, where Christ is, seated at the

right hand of God. Set your minds on things above, not on earthly things" (Colossians 3:1–2).

"Finally, brothers and sisters, whatever is true, whatever is noble, whatever is right, whatever is pure, whatever is lovely, whatever is admirable—if anything is excellent or praiseworthy—think about such things. Whatever you have learned or received or heard from me, or seen in me—put it into practice. And the God of peace will be with you" (Philippians 4:8–9).

However, one may wonder if this level of holiness is even feasible for humans. How can a weak, inadequate human being possibly become complete?

Against such doubts, however, we must remember that God would not leave us with an utterly impossible task.

The Bible warns us that Satan, who uses all sorts of methods to cause people to become distant from God, prowls around like a roaring lion. "Be self-controlled and alert. Your enemy the devil prowls around like a roaring lion looking for someone to devour. Resist him, standing firm in the faith, because you know that your brothers throughout the world are undergoing the same kind of sufferings" (1 Peter 5:8).

Early believers in Christ went through all sorts of persecution and suffered martyrdom in a struggle to keep their faith, but today, Satan knows very well that such a physical and visible strategy to separate people from God will no longer be effective. Early Christians remained true to their faith to the point of martyrdom when it came down to the simple question of whether or not they believed in Jesus. However, many Christians today live in democratic countries with freedom of religion taken for granted. So, in their daily lives, they rarely come face-to-face with situations wherein they must defend their faith with their lives.

That is why Satan uses the trickery of making people's hearts distant from God by luring people with sweet temptations or through crafty disguises—so that they do not notice themselves falling into sin.

Out of the numerous ways of distancing people from God, tools such as distractions, laziness, and business work so effectively that people easily and naturally drift farther and farther away from God. This is why spending our days sitting in front of the TV absorbed in soap operas or being driven by various trivial, worldly temptations will distance our minds from God, making Him an ambiguous, burdensome presence.

The mass media also play a significant role in normalising sin through the skilful disguise of evil by wrapping it up beautifully to deceive the eyes of people. Through novels, films, and dramas that romanticise and justify seemingly beautiful stories of love, which actually have adulterous content and protagonists who engage in murder, deceit, lies, and theft, the media thus infiltrate the values and beliefs of ordinary people, confusing them so that evil is normalised in their lives.

Furthermore, the all-pervasive strategy of using the bandwagon psychology of "everyone does it" causes people to become unhesitant in sinning. As the intelligence and culture of human civilization continue to develop, Satan becomes all the more dexterous, devoting all his energy and strength to keeping humans far away from God. However, people are completely oblivious to this fact.

When a person can't keep awake through God's Words, he or she finds it difficult to distinguish Satan's clever disguises. Even today, Satan tries to plunder our minds. With all his strength, he tries to crumple up the soul. His seductive Mephistophelian waltz deceives people with its sweet melody, capturing them as slaves to sin and breaking up their souls. However, people dance this waltz of death as if they were puppets moving on strings that Mephisto pulls; they do not realise that their souls are heading towards destruction.

Satan is aware that a full-fledged, conspicuous battle is no longer an effective strategy, as it was against early Christians. Thus, in today's world, he uses all sorts of tricks to bamboozle people from believing in God. "Be alert and of sober mind. Your enemy the devil prowls around like a roaring lion looking for someone to devour. Resist him, standing firm in the faith, because you know that the family of believers throughout the world is undergoing the same kind of sufferings" (1 Peter 5:8–9).

A person cannot resist Satan without proper knowledge of the Bible and when standing only on elementary faith. One must spend time with God, reading the Bible and meditating upon it, if he or she is to remain firm against the reprisals of Satan, who prowls like a lion waiting to devour.

Knowing the Bible enables one to know the will of God and act accordingly. If we realise His will and strive to act it out, then the God of peace will surely make us complete in holiness.

In conclusion, Christians must always be praying and staying alert with the Words of God so that they can sufficiently win against Satan, the master of disguise who started as the Serpent that deceived the woman. Having grown in evil and power, the Devil comes back with the authority of a dragon. In order to live a life that doesn't die to evil (which comes disguised in a variety of shapes and sizes), we must arm ourselves thoroughly with the Words of God as our weapon and shield. The Bible, which is the Word of God, is our suit of armour, the shield of truth, and the powerful weapon that will defend us against the temptations of the Devil, and bring us to victory.

> Therefore put on the full armor of God, so that when the day of evil comes, you may be able to stand your ground, and after you have done everything, to stand. Stand firm then, with the belt of truth buckled around your waist, with the breastplate of righteousness in place, and with your feet fitted with the readiness that comes from the gospel of peace. In addition to all this, take up the shield of faith, with which you can extinguish all the flaming arrows of the evil one. Take the helmet of salvation and the sword of the Spirit, which is the word of God. (Ephesians 6:13–17)

In the face of God's glory, we must hold on tightly to the Word of Life and make every effort to become complete. Of course, it is not an easy task to become complete while living in this world, but no matter how difficult it may be, it is surely possible with God's help and grace. In order to help His disciples, Jesus promised them the Holy Spirit (John 20:22; Acts 1:5–8).

Anyone who is in Christ is a new creation (2 Corinthians 5:17). As those who have Jesus' Spirit are His people, we can win over any worldly temptations, since God's Spirit is within us. "I can do anything through Him who gives me strength" (Philippians 4:13).

CHAPTER 36

Christianity and Money

> Keep your lives free from the love of money and be content with what you have, because God has said, "Never will I leave you; never will I forsake you."
>
> —Hebrews 13:5

Money is not a bad thing in itself. But loving it is. Money can be a necessary means of living, but if it becomes an idol or the goal of life itself, then it is better not to have any at all. Loving money is the root of a million sins. If this love branches out, then death will follow.

God wants us to rule over material objects, too. By this, He means that we should be satisfied with our possessions and share them with our needy neighbours instead of being slaves to avarice. Therefore, when we offer up our possessions for the needy, it is the same as lending them to God Himself. If we avoid vanity and extravagance and become frugal, offering our wealth to help others, then God will surely pay us back.

Reading the Bible will change how you regard and value material possessions. A Christian should have the mindset of a faithful steward who uses his or her belongings in a way that God desires and is pleased with. With this attitude, Christians should pay their tithe and help their neighbours who are in need. Paying tithes is an act of recognising that the Lord of our possessions is God. The Bible tells us not to test God but when it comes to paying the tithe, it challenges us to test Him. Those who pay tithes in faith will surely experience the blessings written in the Bible.

> Bring the whole tithe into the storehouse, that there may be food in my house. "Test me in this," says the Lord Almighty, "and see if I will not throw open the floodgates of heaven and pour out so much blessing that you will not have room enough for it. I will prevent pests from devouring your crops, and the vines in your fields will not cast their fruit," says the Lord Almighty. "Then all the nations will call you blessed, for yours will be a delightful land," says the Lord Almighty. (Malachi 3:10–12)
>
> "And do not forget to do good and to share with others, for with such sacrifices God is pleased" (Hebrews 13:16).
>
> "One man gives freely, yet gains even more; another withholds unduly, but comes to poverty" (Proverbs 11:24).

Once we quash the desire of our minds and strive to live by the Bible, God's will fills us up all the more. The things I possess are not truly mine; they have only been entrusted to me while I'm living on the earth. If I mistakenly regard them as wholly mine and handle them according to my avarice and desires, it means I am misusing God's property.

The correct attitude in handling God's entrusted assets is handling them prudently, free from personal greed.

Therefore, we must have an attitude reflecting rational frugality. We mustn't waste our possessions through greed, buy things desirable to the eyes, or be blinded by the pride of life to serve our bodily selves. Also, as Christians, we must have the minds of faithful stewards. By managing our economics so that they are in line with God's intentions, we must serve those who are in poverty and live a life of sharing what we have.

CHAPTER 37

A Three-Dimensional World and Noah's Ark

The story of Noah's ark is so famous that it is known even by people who never once opened up the Bible.

It starts with God's commanding Noah to build an ark three storeys high.

It is as though the three storeys of the ark point to a three-dimensional world and are related to the form of heaven.

From the age of seventy to the age of eighty, Noah poured all his strength into completing the ark. Then, out of the entire earth's population, only he and his eight family members were saved, along with the animals selected by species, according to God's command.

Genesis 7 describes Noah as a righteous man. It is not easy to find many others in the Bible who are described with such words. Also, the Bible tells us that he lived his life walking with God, like his great-grandfather Enoch, who did not die but ascended to heaven.

There are only two people in the entire Bible who ascended to heaven without dying first: Enoch and Elijah.

The Bible tells us that Elijah walked with God for 365 years before he disappeared from the earth because God had taken him.

In striking contrast with today's Sunday Christians, every day of Enoch's life was filled with God.

Like with people who experienced the flood in Noah's times, we are living inundated with a flood of knowledge and information in this contemporary world. We have been swept by the endless waves of information with which the Internet provides us. The power of a popular blogger carries just as strong a force as the mighty blows of warriors in ancient mythologies. The media exert influence that can kill or save lives.

The Internet is advantageous for gaining useful information, but it is more often the case that people surf the Web to find useless information or else use blogs unproductively to criticise and attack others, overall costing time that is precious. Overwhelmed by this tide of information, which causes people to kill time with online gaming or gambling and invades other people's privacy with useless gossip, a soul becomes diseased.

Having time alone to meditate upon the Bible and spend time with God enables the spiritual construction of the ark of one's soul. Piling up one's knowledge of God equates to building up the ark of one's soul. A person with abundant knowledge of God is steady in his or her beliefs and does not easily fall into temptation to sin. However, if a person does not know the Bible, then his or her soul can only drown in the flood of useless information.

God despairs for the people who live in ignorance and who lack understanding. That is why He destroyed the world through the flood. However, after this incident, He showed Noah the band of a rainbow in the sky, promising that He would never again judge the world through water. Through the flood of Noah, we can learn from history that we must put the truth of God's Word before any other knowledge or wisdom in this world.

> "Hear the word of the Lord, you Israelites, because the Lord has a charge to bring against you who live in the land: 'There is no faithfulness, no love, no acknowledgment of God in the land. There is only

> cursing, lying and murder, stealing and adultery; they break all bounds, and bloodshed follows bloodshed'" (Hosea 4:1–2).

> "My people are destroyed from lack of knowledge. Because you have rejected knowledge, I also reject you as my priests; because you have ignored the law of your God, I also will ignore your children" (Hosea 4:6).

When in ignorance of God's truth, a person does not realise that he or she is walking the path to destruction. Even if a Christian lives his or her entire life going to church, it all adds up to nothing if he or she does not understand the Bible.

> "I will not punish your daughters when they turn to prostitution, nor your daughters-in-law when they commit adultery, because the men themselves consort with harlots and sacrifice with shrine prostitutes—a people without understanding will come to ruin" (Hosea 4:14)!

> "Their deeds do not permit them to return to their God. A spirit of prostitution is in their heart; they do not acknowledge the Lord" (Hosea 5:4).

Also, even if a person spends most of his or her life going to church every Sunday, and no matter how much volunteer work or good things a person may have done, if he or she does not understand the Bible, then he or she has no relationship with God.

> "Foreigners sap his strength, but he does not realize it. His hair is sprinkled with grey, but he does not notice" (Hosea 7:9).

> "I wrote for them the many things of my law, but they regarded them as something foreign" (Hosea 8:12).

However, Noah was man of completeness who "did all that God commanded him." If a person is to live an obedient life as Noah did, then he or she must know the Words of God in order to act them out. For this reason, God wants people to know the truth of who He is.

> "For I desire mercy, not sacrifice, and acknowledgment of God rather than burnt offerings" (Hosea 6:6).

> "But I have been the Lord your God ever since you came out of Egypt. You shall acknowledge no God but me, no Savior except me" (Hosea 13:4).

> "Now this is eternal life: that they know you, the only true God, and Jesus Christ, whom you have sent" (John 17:3).

We must grab onto the Words of God and return to Him in order to live our lives and build up the ark of our souls. Noah's ark has not rusted away with history. Its significance remains afloat in our lives today.

CHAPTER 38

Three Principles of Action

God gave us three principles of action. Within these, the secret to a happy life is revealed. First is a life that is lived in joy. Second is unceasing prayer. Third is a life of always giving thanks.

Living in this world, most of us have no joy in our lives. No one is always bright and full of joy. However, in commanding us to rejoice always, God intends for us to live optimistically with complete trust and faith in Him, no matter what the circumstance may be—whether we have reason to be cheerful or sad.

This means that we must always talk with God in our minds. Without prayer, one cannot hope to do well in anything. "Rejoice always, pray continually, give thanks in all circumstances; for this is God's will for you in Christ Jesus. Do not quench the Spirit. Do not treat prophecies with contempt but test them all; hold on to what is good, reject every kind of evil" (1 Thessalonians 5:16–22).

Establishing His justice to humankind through the precious blood of Jesus, God gave us the Holy Spirit as a gift of grace and commanded His people to live uprightly and in holiness. Our bodies are the temple of God, and a gathering of believers is the very community we call church. God works through those who believe in Him, and such believers must live as a breathing confession, saying that Jesus Christ is their Lord of their lives with their lips. Through their lifestyle, they must reveal Christ by pursuing goodness through actions of faithfulness and integrity. "Make sure that nobody pays back wrong for wrong, but always strive to do what is good for each other and for everyone else" (1 Thessalonians 5:15).

Loving your neighbours and always repaying evil with good is easy enough to say but extremely hard to act out. However, if a person meditates on the Bible, living an honest, upright life and treating people with respect and love as though they were God Himself, then the three principles are indeed possible to achieve through His grace.

CHAPTER 39

Knowledge to Eternal Life

> Let us acknowledge the Lord; let us press on to acknowledge him. As surely as the sun rises, he will appear; he will come to us like the winter rains, like the spring rains that water the earth."
>
> —Hosea 6:3

When people are in uncertainty or doubt, the least they can do is investigate the situation to find out the truth. Before they start to deny or accept the fact, they need enough evidence in order to make the final judgement. If they make the wrong decision without knowing all the facts, then they will have to face the consequences later. This is how people sin in ignorance.

Atheists or non-believers shouldn't simply make judgements of Christians based on their outwardly appearance and actions. Instead, they should scrutinise the words of the Bible. As the Israelites spread the blood of a lamb on their doorposts during the Passover before Exodus, we have gained redemption from the judgement of death through the blood of Jesus. Also, in the way that the Israelites had their cloaks tucked into their belts and hurriedly ate the Passover food, we must take in the Words of God swiftly when we are at critical moments in our lives. That is how we can avoid the judgement of death.

Furthermore, during the Passover, the Israelites ate bread without yeast. This signifies how we should take in God's truth without adding anything to it. We should take in His Words just as they are. In order to survive this corrupt world, we must arm ourselves with God's truth. If we do not face up to evil, equipped with His truth, then we will be overcome before we know it.

The nature of this spiritual battle is completely different from fights and brawls between humans. We must become warriors of faith whom the world cannot withstand, and we must ultimately win the battle against evil. That is the kind of life a disciple of Jesus should lead. Loving God, doing no harm to one's neighbours, not seeking vengeance against one's enemies, and overcoming evil with good is proper conduct for a Christian.

Acts of visible evil fall under the general standards of morals and ethics in this world, which non-Christians and atheists follow. However, the battle we are engaged in is one that is beyond the visible dimension of ordinary ethics: We must defeat evil in our minds. Jesus' teaching that simply hating one's brother in the mind equates to murder and avarice amounts to committing theft tells us that we must purify ourselves from the inside out. Winning the fight against the world means fulfilling Christ's love in one's life, ridding the self of evil such as selfishness, jealousy, and avarice.

A visible enemy is easy to defeat. However, an enemy in disguise is difficult to single out. The Bible tells us that Satan disguises himself as an angel of light. To fend off this trickery, though, the Bible tells us the standards to differentiate good and evil. It teaches that our minds as well as our actions should become undefiled and pure. If we know the Bible, we will be able to distinguish whether our minds, thoughts, or intentions are bent on good or evil. "For the word of God is alive and active. Sharper than any double-edged sword, it penetrates even to dividing soul and spirit, joints and marrow; it judges the thoughts and attitudes of the heart. Nothing in all creation is hidden from God's sight. Everything is uncovered and laid bare before the eyes of him to whom we must give account" (Hebrews 4:12–13).

God, who lives eternally, speaks to us today through the Bible. He earnestly desires for us to gain realisation and understanding through His truth and take the path of eternal life.

> Finally, be strong in the Lord and in his mighty power. Put on the full armour of God, so that you can take your stand against the devil's schemes. For our struggle is not against flesh and blood, but against the rulers, against the authorities, against the powers of this dark world and against the spiritual forces of evil in the heavenly realms. Therefore put on the full armour of God, so that when the day of evil comes, you may be able to stand your ground, and after you have done everything, to stand. Stand firm then, with the belt of truth buckled around your waist, with the breastplate of righteousness in place, and with your feet fitted with the readiness that comes from the gospel of peace. In addition to all this, take up the shield of faith, with which you can extinguish all the flaming arrows of the evil one. Take the helmet of salvation and the sword of the Spirit, which is the word of God. (Ephesians 6:10–17)

If a person out in the battlefield has no sword, then he or she no longer has the means to fight. Without the sword of God's truth, we cannot hope to fight against the evil in the world. That is why we must know the Bible first and foremost, before any knowledge or wisdom of the world. The Bible, the compilation of God's truth, is an amazing book that works in people's lives in ways that are individualized, unique to each person and situation. The Bible is a force of change that transforms people's minds and lives. It is filled with words of God's amazing power. When a person gains understanding from these words and starts to live in upright holiness and reverence of the Father as His son or daughter, his or her life becomes one that gives glory to God.

Knowing the Bible is, conclusively, the way to eternal life.

CHAPTER 40

The Purpose of Creation

> The people I formed for myself that they may proclaim my praise.
>
> —Isaiah 43:21

The purpose of creation was for God to receive glory. But when the first human, Adam, sinned and brought along the fall of humankind, God's glory was shunned from the world, which grew into a place of evil filled with lament and suffering (Romans 8:22). The world became more and more corrupt until humans fell into a state of spiritual ignorance, unknowing of God's existence.

With the true purpose and meaning of life lost to humanity, many spend a lifetime chasing the false goal of happiness until they pass away one day. Even though an afterlife obviously exists, those who deny or live in ignorance of this fact and, instead, live out their lives compromising their consciences for the affluence and wants of the world end up drawing their last breath in vain, the total worth of their lifetime not even amounting to a single day.

All humans seek happiness. There is probably not a single person who doesn't want to be happy. The desire for and pursuit of happiness in this lifetime or some kind of afterlife is the common ground of interest for all people.

Aristotle defined happiness as a state of being wherein one is satisfied with oneself, but the truth is that the nature of the fallen person does not know true satisfaction and craves for unlimited wants and desires. This is why people cannot be pleased with themselves and chase after the false ideals of happiness, losing sense of what it truly embodies.

Happiness cannot be guaranteed, no matter how successful a person may be. While acquiring a grand title, power, affluence, or gain may offer temporary comfort, it cannot amount to true happiness. Through such worldly means, one cannot gain satisfaction of the soul or the eternal afterlife.

Solomon, who was the king during Israel's golden years, possessed all the wealth and honour a man could possibly hold. He had brilliant wisdom and knew the secrets of all creation. Even so, towards the end of his life, he confessed that everything in the world was meaningless. He compared all knowledge, titles, wealth, and honour acquired during his lifetime to trying to catch the wind.

In his book Ecclesiastes, Solomon repeatedly proclaims that life is meaningless from start to finish. He says that everyone has a certain "time" in their lives in which God fulfils His wondrous works and that people cannot possibly estimate when this will be. That is why God gave us hearts that long for eternity. King Solomon claimed that there is nothing better in life than to rejoice while living and doing good works.

All of this is embodied in the three principle actions given to humanity by God. "He has made everything beautiful in its time. He has also set eternity in the human heart; yet no one can fathom what God has done from beginning to end. I know that there is nothing better for people than to be happy and to do good while they live" (Ecclesiastes 3:11–12).

In the final chapter of Ecclesiastes, Solomon concludes that one who remembers his Creator in the days of his youth has life that holds true value. The life Solomon saw as valuable is one that remembers its Creator, which is ultimately the purpose of creation itself. "Remember your Creator in the days of your youth, before the days of trouble come and the years approach when you will say, 'I find no pleasure in them'" (Ecclesiastes12:1).

The original intention for God's creation of humankind was to exalt them high. Similarly, a life lived according to the ultimate purpose for a humankind exalts God. People who live in accordance to this reason for creation are practitioners of love who follow Jesus Christ as an example in their human relationships. Thus, they live a life that is selfless and that shines in brilliance as an example to others.

Therefore, God wants you to know your true purpose for being. The Bible is God's heartfelt letter that delivers the news of His salvation and love for humankind. The letter holds God's will and emotions from the heart. It is through this letter that we can open our eyes and see God. So let us make every effort in getting to know the Bible, a book that contains all answers for life.

PART FIVE

Reassessing the Mirror

PART FIVE

Reassessing the Mirror

In March 2012, I was catching up with a friend who is an editor of one of Korea's major newspapers. He said he was Catholic but hadn't yet read the Bible. As I told him, "If someone like you read the Bible, you would understand it much better than I do," it occurred to me that I should write a book about how my life had been transformed through the Word of God. I was inspired to write a testimony for "Christians" who had never once read through the Bible.

CHAPTER 41

The Wilderness Walk

From my unexpected divorce up to the pen incident, my new life as a Christian had been a tumultuous time of discovery. With newfound faith in God, I'd adjusted to foreign surroundings in England and expanded the frontiers of my spiritual life. I'd received God's mercy and learned more about my Maker. I'd battled against my circumstances and my own sinful nature. I'd been broken, humbled, and moved by the melody of His saving grace as I was brought to tears by the softly sung hymns of the St. G. Church choir.

However, I had left St. G. Church disappointed and disheartened after the pen incident. For years, I sailed another voyage through dark and murky waters, embarking on a new stage of spiritual learning and maturity. Going beyond "individualistic faith," I learned what it truly means to live and grow as a Christian amidst the dark corners of community and the daily struggles of life.

I found a Korean church near New Malden, a town in southern London where many Koreans live. I attended and served at the church for about four years before moving to another Korean church for my two final years in England. My years in the Korean ministries were probably the most dynamic experience of my spiritual life, as I came face-to-face with unexpected challenges, both good and bad, within the community.

Through the discipleship training programme at my church, I grew closer to God by studying His Word and learning His verses by heart. I even read theological texts and books on science and philosophy to seek out more and more about my Creator. I also started accompanying the choir and became more involved in church life, participating in the women's ministry and attending Wednesday services.

However, as I became more involved in the small community, I began to uncover the dark areas of community life. There was a great amount of bickering, gossiping, and negative sentiments between the members. After service, the congregation became segmented into cliques, with gossip, backbiting, jealousy, and malice filling in the cracks. The more I stayed in that vitriolic environment, the more I became disheartened, feeling myself being sucked into the spew of ungodliness within the church. I witnessed conflicts over power and money, and I saw pure jealousy. I once became a victim of gossip myself, for reasons I don't understand to this day. I was confused and hurt and began to wonder what it truly meant to live a Christian life.

Unfortunately, infighting and divisions are common phenomena that infect the modern-day church, preventing it from becoming a healthy, united body of Christ. Such hypocritical behaviour both discourages believers and repels non-believers from becoming part of the Christian community. Churchgoers preach of love, peace, and community, yet they seem to act the very opposite.

What difference is there between non-believers and those who go to church yet who often lie, cheat others, and go around gossiping about other people? In a spiritual community, believers must share words of grace, encouragement, and thanksgiving, and refrain from slandering or criticising others. If fellow believers of Christ cannot love each other and instead bicker and show hostility towards one another, then how can they deliver the gospel?

True faith is not only about listening to the truth of the gospel. It is about actually transforming our minds and living out the truth. However, many so-called believers do not experience any spiritual betterment. Still, they use verses from the Bible to cut others down with criticism.

What's more, the different branches of the church actually slander each other for not having the same doctrines, each group insisting on its own righteousness.

Could it honestly be right to insist on one's own righteousness while throwing away the love and tolerance of God?

A life of faith in God should not be based on criticising other religions or obsessing over Christian doctrine and practice. A life of faith is about knowing God and devoting our lives to follow His will for us. Discouraging other believers and causing non-believers to be repelled by a life of hypocrisy makes the faith of a "churchgoer" questionable.

In this regard, the book of James tells us the following:

> "Do not merely listen to the word, and so deceive yourselves. Do what it says" (James 1:22).
>
> "What good is it, my brothers and sisters, if someone claims to have faith but has no deeds? Can such faith save them" (James 2:14)?
>
> "In the same way, faith by itself, if it is not accompanied by action, is dead; As the body without the spirit is dead, so faith without deeds is dead" (James 2:17,26).

What follows the faith of a person's salvation should be the spiritual maturity and transformation of one's lives, after committing oneself to following Jesus. Salvation is not about having everything in life go swimmingly or about receiving a free VIP ticket to heaven.

Salvation is living a blessed life that understands the love of God, walking in fellowship with Him and obeying His Word through the Holy Spirit.

If we live our lives in this way, under God's guidance and His will, then we are in fellowship with Him—and this is ultimately the life we will have in heaven. Thus, if we live with this blessing, we already have the kingdom of heaven within us.

With these contemplations, I was able to break free from the hurt I received from others at church. I also began to pray for God's wisdom to discern His will and to live a life that followed the love of Christ by tolerating others instead of repaying evil with evil.

God wants us to live a fruitful life bearing integrity, peace, tolerance, and gentleness, without prejudice and deceit. However, this is easier said than done. We, as humans, find ourselves flying into temper tantrums and acting out of our own selfish desires. That is why in Romans 7:19, Paul said, "I do not do the good I want to do, but the evil I do not want to do—this I keep on doing." He exclaimed, "What a wretched man I am," in verse 24. Even spiritual figures like Paul became frustrated with this human dilemma of occasionally slipping off the path of following Jesus. It is not an easy journey. However, God requires faith from us. "I am God Almighty; walk before me faithfully and be blameless" (Genesis 17:1).

If we have faith, then we must live with the aim of making it complete through our actions. We must live as though we are in the presence of God, doing our best to live upright lives with no deceit, regardless of who may be watching. If we try to live this way in integrity and conscientiousness, then God will constantly supply us with His wisdom and guard our thoughts and minds at all times. This is the life of a true Christian.

CHAPTER 42

Intertwined in Faith

A tree cannot stand on its own. Its roots must be intertwined with those of other trees in order to brace against thunder or storms that may knock it down.

Having been an independent drifter for all my life, I had never been deeply involved in any group activity, even when I was at university. With my lack of social experience, I became rather disappointed and jaded by my experience in the Korean ministry in England. When I returned to Korea, I began working in concert planning and management, so my individualism returned and I stuck to watching sermons on the Internet and church-hopping, as I was reluctant to commit to a community. I did not realise then the necessity of having a community in order to stand strong in faith.

For almost three years, I worked tirelessly in concert planning and even performed myself along with an orchestra in both Korea and London. Although I wasn't committed to a church, I still felt God's grace working in my life, allowing me to experience a rewarding work life for the first time. For that I was grateful.

At the same time, without a source of living water or a community of faith, I found myself falling farther away from a life of holiness. I was obsessed with my job. I moved up the career ladder and even ended up working for the former president of Korea. However, I found myself living out each day in aggressiveness and worldliness rather than living out a Christian life of wisdom and good character.

Spiritually burned out and physically worn out, I finally became humbled to respond to God's call to take a step back. I decided to leave my job and wondered what it was that God wanted me to do. Visiting my elderly parents every other day, practicing the piano, and committing to a church were just simple goals that I came up with.

Living a simpler, more humble life, I recovered from physical and spiritual fatigue. I began to regularly attend an Anglican church in Seoul and became involved in fellowship. I actually stayed after service for the first time and got to know the people. I began to see the bigger picture of being in a community. Of course, I still saw the differences between us, the mannerisms and our human faults and weaknesses. I realised that although we are not complete, we are together, being built into the unity of God's love. "From him the whole body, joined and held together by every supporting ligament, grows and builds itself up in love, as each part does its work" (Ephesians 4:16).

Being part of a community is about sharing God's love and blessings with others. It is about encouraging others and, in turn, being encouraged and strengthened. I enjoyed blessing others and motivating them with words. I also wanted to share and bless others with my love for music. A few months into the ministry, I found the heart to start serving as a music director and, two years later, as a teacher for the high school ministry.

Each week, I remember the beauty of community in Christ as I serve, have fellowship, and partake in the Holy Communion. I've finally realised that it is a community that helps you live out a true Christian life as you struggle with the grievances of daily life, of work, and ultimately of the person you see in the mirror.

CHAPTER 43

A Blessed Life

Reflecting back on my years of adolescent defiance and also on my middle years of knowing and trying to follow God, I can see that every twist and turn in my life showed the patterns of God's grace. Every day, I get to know and understand Him more and more, little by little. But it is amazing to me that He knew everything about me before the creation of the earth.

When my marriage was falling apart and finally caved in, God saved me from my living death. Beyond this act of mercy, He granted me with a new life with wonders I could have never imagined: freedom from my fears, anxiety, and depression, and release from my vented anger and hatred. Beyond extending His mercy and grace, He has even allowed things I never could have accomplished in my old life, such as working in concert management (when I'd never worked a day in my life) and performing as a concert pianist in London's and Korea's biggest music halls. God blessed me with desires of my heart I never dared to ask for. What God intended all along was the salvation of my soul.

Focusing on God and acknowledging Him in our daily lives is easier than we might expect. An abundant life of peace and unexpected pleasures is what follows. This life comes once we entrust our own lives to God under His will and guidance. In this sense, I feel like a blessed person, and I try to live in thanksgiving and gratitude to God.

"Blessed is the one who does not walk in step with the wicked or stand in the way that sinners take or sit in the company of mockers, but whose delight is in the law of the Lord, and who meditates on his law day and night." Psalm 1 does not identify blessed people as those with money or might but instead defines them as those who do not follow evil and who humble themselves to receiving God's Words in their lives. A person who delights in God's Words, contemplating and putting them into practice, is like a "tree by streams of water."

God gives us a happiness that satisfies the thirst of the soul. Day by day, drawing close and knowing Him more and more makes joy and thanksgiving overflow from the soul. In this way, being joyful in thanksgiving is what God desires from us. That is why I read the Bible every day and have allotted time for prayer. Without this daily devotion, the remnants of my inherent nature resurface. I get angry and irritated over small matters and say hurtful things to the people around me. But then, despite my human shortcomings, I open the book again and, with reflection and prayer, am filled with the strength to start over again. When I fret over whether I will live with the roots of pride and hatred all my life, I receive comfort as I remember Jacob, our spiritual ancestor.

I recall the episode where Jacob wrestles until dawn with the angel by the Jabbok River. Jacob was given the name "Israel," which signifies the one "who struggled with God and with humans and has overcome." Through this episode, I felt God comforting me, indicating that although a person may seem stuck in a lifelong struggle of inherently sinful nature and disbelieving actions, He still accepts us as "His people," like the Israelites who sinned against God time and time again.

However, walking the path of life with God and experiencing His profound love, I live in hope that we will become transformed like Enoch and that the grace of God will complete us. We walk without knowing of the things to come, but I believe that if we live in thankfulness of His guidance and grace, then He will most certainly transform our lives.

Sources

Scripture quotations are taken from the *Holy Bible: New International Version®*. *NIV®*. Copyright © 1973, 1978, 1984 by International Bible Society. Used by permission of Zondervan. All rights reserved.

Chapter 3: The Silence of God

[1] Born, M. *The Born–Einstein Letters: Friendship, Politics and Physics in Uncertain Times*. New York: Palgrave Macmillan, 1971.

Part Two: The Problem of Pain

[1] Lewis, C. S. *The Problem of Pain*. London: HarperCollins, 2002.

Chapter 25: The Mind of God

[1] Hawking, Stephen. *A Brief History of Time*. New York: Bantam, 1998.
[2] Kaku, Michio. *Hyperspace: A Scientific Odyssey through Parallel Universes, Time Warps and the Tenth Dimension*. Oxford: Oxford University Press, 1995.

Chapter 31: The Human Error

[1] Dawkins, Richard. *The God Delusion*. Boston: Houghton Mifflin Co., 2006.
[2] Kaku, op. cit.

Chapter 32: Understanding beyond Our Dimension

[1] Davies, Paul. *The Mind of God: Science and the Search for Ultimate Meaning*. New York: Simon & Schuster, 1992.